Get Set for Study in the UK

Titles in the GET SET FOR UNIVERSITY series:

Get Set for American Studies
ISBN 0 7486 1692 6

Get Set for English Language
ISBN 0 7486 1544 X

Get Set for English Literature
ISBN 0 7486 1537 7

Get Set for Geography
ISBN 0 7486 1693 4

Get Set for Linguistics
ISBN 0 7486 1694 2

Get Set for Media Studies
ISBN 0 7486 1695 0

Get Set for Philosophy
ISBN 0 7486 1657 8

Get Set for Politics
ISBN 0 7486 1545 8

Get Set for Study in the UK
ISBN 0 7486 1810 4

Get Set for Study in the UK

Tom Barron

Edinburgh University Press

© Tom Barron, 2003

Edinburgh University Press Ltd
22 George Square, Edinburgh

Typeset in Sabon
by Hewer Text Ltd, Edinburgh, and
printed and bound in Finland by
WS Bookwell

A CIP record for this book is
available from the British Library

ISBN 0 7486 1810 4 (paperback)

CONTENTS

PREFACE

If you are intending to become an international student in the UK, this book is addressed to you. But it is not the kind of book which you should try to read from cover to cover. It deals with all levels of study (undergraduate, postgraduate and study abroad) and different kinds of studies (taught and research) and not all sections will be of use to you immediately. It is designed to allow you to skim through the contents and to note the titles of chapters and sections. You can then decide which parts interest you and can safely ignore the rest, though you may want to come back to what you have missed later, as your needs change. No guide can cover every possible situation which students are likely to face. That is why there are questions at the end of each chapter which invite you to think out how the matters discussed relate to your own circumstances. Academic terms in bold are explained in the Glossary.

Studying abroad can be exciting, deeply rewarding and enlightening. It can also be challenging and stressful. This book has been devised for anyone who has an interest in studying abroad but knows little of the mechanics or the opportunities and the pitfalls involved. It attempts to suggest ways of anticipating the issues which arise when you decide to study abroad and to provide suggestions about how best to deal with them. Primarily, the guide's subject is education in the UK, though much of what is said may be of interest even to those contemplating studying in other locations. It deals with tertiary education, principally higher education, though it may again be of interest to those contemplating studying in other areas. It is intended primarily for students, and for parents, teachers, counsellors, agents and government officials who give advice about, fund and support those who plan to study abroad. Its main purpose is to consider what students themselves want to know and what they are likely to need to know. The aim is to enable both students and their advisers to feel confident about their understanding of what is involved and so to get set for study in the UK.

This guide to study in the UK looks at the whole process of becoming an international student, from first considering the possibility through to undertaking the studies. It endeavours to see this from the point of view of the mobile student and to provide clear information and helpful advice. It is written by someone with a strong belief in the benefits which international education can bring and in the hope that in future more students will be able to experience them. The intention is to remove something of the confusion and uncertainty which often surrounds the subject. If the book succeeds in that and if it helps you to make up your mind to study abroad and to feel confident in undertaking your studies, it will have served its purpose.

PART I
Getting Set

1 WHY STUDY IN THE UK?

STUDYING ABROAD

Wherever you live in the world, you have the opportunity today to study outside your own country. To decide to take up that opportunity, however, requires thought and planning. It also requires spirit and courage to break free from the easier alternative of staying at home. And it is not a decision to be made lightly. Studying abroad involves a considerable commitment of time, energy and funds. Its rewards are great but so also is the investment that needs to be made in it, personally, socially, academically, financially. The more thought you give to it in advance, the more confident you can be that the investment really is worthwhile.

THE CHOICE

If you are intending to study abroad, it is first necessary to choose a country in which to study. Nowadays the choice is great. Most countries can accommodate international students and many have made special arrangements to do so. The result is an enormous diversity of provision. Some of what is on offer is open only to English-speakers. This is true of the United States, which constitutes the biggest receiving country for international students, and it is true of the other anglophone countries, particularly the UK and Australia, which admit very large numbers. But some courses in English specifically aimed at international students are also available in a number of non-anglophone countries. In a few of these countries English is sufficiently widely understood as a second or third language as to enable other aspects of normal daily life, like buying food or

3

finding a place to stay, to be conducted in that language, too. For those with skills in other languages, there are also opportunities to study abroad alongside local students in a great many more non-anglophone countries, such as Germany, France, Russia or Japan. The huge choice of destinations can be intimidating and no country is going to be exactly right for everybody. Each is different and each has its own strengths. But it is possible to narrow down the choice by looking further into what each country offers and by assessing your own interests and needs. Everyone is likely to have a personal agenda and a unique perspective. If you know what your reasons are for wishing to study abroad, your hopes and expectations, and you also know what study opportunities are available, you are in a position to make the choice.

WHY CHOOSE THE UK?

The UK is one of the principal destinations for internationally mobile students. Those who choose the UK say that it offers a number of advantages. Its **higher education** system is centuries old and it is regarded as high in quality. It is to the UK that many of the other educational systems in the rest of the world owe their origins. This means that UK education is widely known and its value widely understood. It provides a transferable currency: qualifications that are recognised and respected in a great many countries in the world. The educational system is also rooted in a culture that places a high value on the pursuit of quality in education, and government in the UK is committed to maintaining the provision of top-quality education as a national goal. When Prime Minister Tony Blair was asked on election to say what the three main themes of his administration would be, he replied: 'Education, education, education.' This stress on educational quality is not, of course, unique. But it does help to explain why Britain has built up a reputation as one of the world's leading suppliers of international education.

Once, western educationalists believed that what they

should teach was classical knowledge – a fundamental cultural understanding, deriving from ancient Greek and Roman learning, which, it was felt, would serve graduates in every situation in life. Today the belief is that education needs to be cutting-edge, dynamic, diverse. Nothing now is considered static or eternal in education. Lifelong learning and continuing professional development, keeping up to date with the very latest knowledge and adapting that knowledge to newly emerging fields, are the current goals. These are certainly the goals that are prized in the UK, by the government, educational authorities, business and the public. They share the responsibility for ensuring that the quality of UK education is maintained. The government expects education to be sensitive to the wishes of the public and to the needs of society and the economy. Its role is to co-ordinate educational policies, to set targets and to provide support, particularly funding support, for achieving the agreed goals. Business's role is partly to indicate the knowledge and skills which future employees will need to have. Business also expects to benefit directly from the knowledge which higher education generates, which explains why companies contribute independently to the educational institutions. The media, too, takes a considerable interest in the educational system and UK newspapers often devote a whole section to it. All this helps to create a strong impetus for achievement from outside as well as within the education sector. It ensures that in the UK high standards for educational development are set and maintained.

MAIN CHARACTERISTICS OF UK HIGHER EDUCATION

To describe something as large and diverse as UK education is not easy. Two of its principal characteristics are that it is personal and practical. There is a clear recognition in Britain that education is central to the development of each individual and fundamental to the productive capacity of every state. You are meant to derive from your studies a sense of personal satisfaction. The goal is a growth not simply in your knowledge but in your understanding. Purely rote learning is less valued in the UK. There is a keen appreciation that education must be dynamic and must foster originality. The intention is to produce graduates who have a sense of mastery over the material they have studied and so a flexibility in being able to apply that learning in different practical contexts. But all this is held equally to be of benefit to society, since a well-educated workforce with flexible understanding and a creative potential is thought necessary to drive on economic growth. There is also in the UK an emphasis on requiring education to be cost-effective. Relatively few students drop out before completing their **course**; fewer still complete the course and then fail to graduate. There are a number of institutions that cater to more occasional students whose studies are less continuous, separated by periods spent gaining work experience. These form an exception to the rule. But, in general, once admitted, you proceed to graduation by gradual and defined stages, each carefully structured to ensure that you are attaining the required goals. Of course, this smooth progress is partly explained by the fact that UK students are very carefully selected, and that can be a hurdle.

Self-learning

Perhaps the aspect of British education most commented upon elsewhere is its emphasis on self-learning. In all teaching there must inevitably be some strongly didactic element, when the student is absorbing what the teacher wishes to convey. But in the UK this has traditionally been supplemented by a belief that if education is to try to foster originality and creativity, you must also be encouraged to learn for yourself. One aspect of self-learning for most undergraduate students is the emphasis put on tutorials or small-group work, where the teacher is able to check your understanding of underlying concepts while encouraging you to communicate with your fellow students. In turn, you share your perceptions with the tutor and with the other students, so that a fuller understanding of the problems under review can be gained. Learning in this way, it is thought, also helps to develop a number of transferable skills, including self-expression, the ability to frame and present an argument effectively and to interact with others in order to reach an agreed conclusion. Together with the skills developed in independent written work, which again involve thinking and expression, this personalised approach to education carries you beyond your immediate discipline into the area of life skills. It can also help to create a stronger sense of academic community, with the teachers and students engaged together in a common search for improved understanding.

Teaching and research

In its higher education, Britain gives emphasis both to teaching skills and research output. In some ways, these are seen as two sides of the same coin. The best teachers are held to be those actively undertaking research. They can guide students towards the educational frontier, communicate an enthusiasm for new knowledge which research brings and keep their teaching fresh and alive with examples drawn from the latest discoveries. But equally, the best researchers are held to be those who undertake teaching. This ensures that the research they conduct informs their teaching, is intelligible to each new generation of students and is in touch with the needs of the wider society from which the students come. British academic staff are therefore encouraged to undertake both research and teaching. Indeed, Britain was the first country to produce an independent system of quality inspection of university teaching and research, based on peer review, aimed not just at maintaining high standards but at fostering innovation and development.

Facilities

Countries which hope to attract international students, particularly those like the UK which emphasise self-learning, are also aware of the importance of providing good facilities. Students need libraries that are well stocked and that can provide access to new sources of information provision, like electronic databases and the World Wide Web. They need to work with the latest equipment, so that they can cope with whatever they encounter in the workplace when they find a job. They need a space to study in and a supportive culture which values that activity. As Britain sets a high store by education, the provision of such facilities is also prized. The equipment available is a feature of the quality inspections and there is government and private funding to ensure that its quality is maintained. The link between research and teaching is a further reason to ensure that the latest equipment is available and also helps to explain why the UK is a major world supplier of educational technology. One fundamental aspect of technological support is bibliographical. Every student spends time studying in a library. All UK universities have major library resources and several have libraries that are considered major world repositories. And these are not the only book resources open to students. There are also public and professional libraries in all the main cities and towns to which students, and other members of the community, often have access.

Quality recognition

For students, the ultimate purpose of higher education is, of course, to gain a qualification. While the nature of that qualification is clearly important, particularly the knowledge gained and the skills mastered, it is equally important that its value is recognised by others. The qualification should be seen not only as evidence of achievement but also as a badge of quality. The British educational system gained its very wide currency in the rest of the world by example. Its currency has grown as UK graduates have gone on to prove their worth, often internationally, in their subsequent careers. But it is also a reflection of the quality controls within UK higher education. British **degrees** are awarded by individual institutions yet each of them ensures that its standards are maintained by a system which brings the voice of 'external' examiners into play. External examiners (**'externals'**) are scholars drawn from other institutions, chosen for their reputation in the field, able to judge standards and required to advise on how those standards should be maintained. Of course, the reputation of the individual institution remains important and that will, inevitably, vary. But, for the education system as a whole, there is a guarantee of minimum achievement standards with each degree, something that the public, employers and government agencies worldwide understand and respect. If in doubt, a check should be made to ensure that the UK degree which interests you is also recognised by the government or professional bodies in the country in which you intend to work. But the chances are high that it will be.

Studying in English

The UK's higher education is offered in English. Today, English is the world's preferred language for international communications. It is the first language in the USA, Canada, Australia and New Zealand as well as in the UK. In the non-anglophone world, it is almost invariably the second language. It is the language of business, of air transport, of academic world congresses, of much of science and medicine, of the international media. And the UK is the home of this language. While some of the principal writers in English – novelists, poets, philosophers – are now found in all continents, the UK remains a major influence on the development of the language everywhere. Very large numbers of students come to the UK every year to study English as a foreign language and to immerse themselves in the culture of the community in which that language was born and where it is used in everyday discourse. A degree in English can therefore have for some a double value, as evidence of mastery of a discipline and as evidence of fluency in the world's principal language.

Subject range

The range and depth of educational provision in the UK is a
further reason often given for studying there. The subjects
available for study spread across all the major areas of academic study worldwide and different approaches are provided
to studying them. Some institutions offer a 'training for the
mind', emphasising the need to understand the theoretical
basis of the discipline. Others are more purely vocational and
emphasise applied learning. But all attempt to blend both of
these features to some degree. Inter-disciplinarity and multi-
disciplinarity (encouraging students to appreciate different
approaches to the same subject and to see links between
different subjects) are also major goals. It has been from
blending knowledge drawn from different disciplines that
some of the most exciting academic discoveries of recent times
have sprung and new disciplines have arisen. Some individual
institutions cater for this by attempting to be comprehensive,
offering for study a very large number of different disciplines.
Others try to be more specialised, by bringing together cognate
disciplines so as to cultivate a reputation in particular areas of
study. But both offer a high degree of choice. Students looking
for a wider understanding of their discipline or who wish to
keep open their options for the future will find this range of
choice helpful.

DEGREE STRUCTURES

If the search is for traditional academic courses, there is a huge
variety on offer, of different lengths and different content,
often requiring different entry qualifications. Every student
contemplating study in the UK needs to begin by getting some
kind of handle on this variety. The basic structure, however, is
quite simple and will be readily familiar to most students
wherever they have been studying. There is normally an
undergraduate degree (sometimes called a first degree and
usually bearing the title Bachelor – though some exceptions

here will be considered later), then an intermediate degree (usually called a master's degree – though there are several different sorts of Master) and finally an advanced degree (which is usually a doctorate). In general, the first degree lasts three or four years, the second one or two years and the third three years or more. This is a pattern found in many international systems. The European Union is currently seeking to entrench this structure throughout all its member countries. Within this basic structure, there are, however, some important distinctions.

Taught degrees

Most undergraduate degrees are primarily taught degrees, meaning that they are delivered mainly by lectures, though you are also required to do independent work and group work, usually in essays, dissertations and tutorials or, in scientific-based study, in practicals and laboratory work. Often, however, the taught element varies, being greater at the start of the degree than in the later stages, when individual learning is more encouraged. Most master's degrees will involve a certain amount of taught work and, compared to first (or bachelor) degrees, a rather larger amount of independent research work. Some master's put the emphasis on the former, some the latter. Those with a large taught element are likely to be identified as 'taught degrees', whereas those intended to provide a grounding in research methodology and practice are likely to classified as 'research degrees'. Advanced master's and doctoral degrees involve a good deal of independent research, but they normally have a taught element, too, usually providing an introduction to the nature of the subject being studied and the methods employed in research. And though nearly all doctoral degrees involve primarily research work, there are even some – if so far only a very, very few – which are mainly taught degrees.

Length of degrees

Not only are the structures different, so are the periods of study and the content of the courses. In England, Wales and Northern Ireland most bachelor degrees last three years; in Scotland some last three years but most take four. Even in England, Wales and Northern Ireland, however, some bachelor degrees involve a period of study outside the university or **college**, in work placements or in language-learning overseas, for example. As a result, these degrees may take four years. Since this feature is also found in Scotland, Scottish degrees of this form can take five years to complete. In both cases, too, there are professional undergraduate degree programmes – in medicine or veterinary medicine, for example – which are longer than the standard degree, quite often five or six years. At the master's level, the UK offers a large number of intensive one-year (twelve months) 'taught' programmes, some one-year (twelve months) 'research' programmes and several two-year (both 'research and taught') master's. Doctoral degrees usually last three years, though the evidence suggests that there is a more open-ended nature to advanced research programmes and not all students do complete their degrees in the minimum period. Doctoral students need to be aware that extra time may be necessary for the writing-up to be completed and the work submitted.

ANGLO-SCOTTISH DIFFERENCES

The differences between the Scottish and the other UK systems often lead to misunderstandings. Scotland was once a separate country and by the time of its political union with England in 1707 an educational system with its own characteristics had developed there. The differences persisted through the long years of union. Since 1999 and the creation of a devolved legislature in Scotland, the differences have begun again to grow. They are most marked at the undergraduate level, though this in turn depends on differences in secondary (or high) schools. English students tend to specialise from around the age of 16, typically taking usually three subjects thereafter and pursuing these for a further two years. Scottish education goes on emphasising the need to retain a breadth of knowledge from age 16, so that a student is more usually studying five subjects, and it normally takes a maximum of two further years before the student moves to university. Indeed it is possible for Scottish students to decide to move to university after only one further year of study, when aged as young as 17 – though this is now rather rare in practice. In recent years some of these distinctions have been eroded by the adoption of AS levels (which resemble Highers) in England and Advanced Highers (which resemble A levels) in Scotland. Differences do remain, however.

As a result of these differences, the first year in Scottish universities tends to require students to spread their studies over a number of different disciplines, whereas in England specialisation is more common from the start. Scottish students decide on their specialist subject or subjects after trying out a number of options, sometimes waiting till the end of their second year before deciding finally, though by then the choice will have become narrowed down. It is also possible for students to avoid making the choice altogether. 'General' or 'ordinary' or 'pass' degree students simply complete a third year, again pursuing a variety of disciplines, and then graduate. But the bulk of Scottish students do opt for the specialist route and remain at their studies until a fourth year to take an 'honours' degree. One Scottish university even offers an honours degree in general subjects by adding a fourth year to the pattern of the first three. Another curious feature of the Scottish system is that the title 'Master' is sometimes used in the older universities for undergraduate degrees in arts and social sciences. Though only the separate historical evolution of these degrees can explain their titles, a good deal of contemporary popular feeling now enters into the debate about whether or not the titles should be changed. Despite all these variations at the undergraduate level, however, Scottish-English differences are much less marked at master's and doctoral levels, where a similar pattern operates in both countries.

PUBLIC AND PRIVATE EDUCATION

International students often ask if a British university is public or private. The answer – that virtually all British universities are public – comes as a surprise to many, particularly those who know that there is a flourishing private sector in schools education in the UK. The one higher education exception – the University of Buckingham – was set up as the harbinger of a new era of private higher education which has never in fact materialised. But instead all the public universities have come to act largely as private ones – undertaking advertising and recruitment, charging 'full fees' to all but 'home' students and seeking to generate income which is not dependent on government funding. Moreover, recent government policy has introduced even 'home' students to the notion of paying fees, either up front, before commencing studies, or in the form of a graduate charge, levied after they enter employment. In neither case, of course, are home students paying 'full' fees, since it is supposed that they (and their parents) make an additional contribution to the state provision of education through the taxation system. However, viewed in this light, it is now arguable that the distinction between public and private universities in the UK is, particularly for international students from outside the European Union, no longer easy to make.

EXTRAMURAL LIFE

If you are thinking of studying abroad, there is more to consider than simply finding a subject, choosing an academic approach or gaining transferable skills. You must be concerned about life outside the classroom and what are often called life-skills. In the UK, this reflects a well-established notion that education must serve 'the whole man' (nowadays we would say 'the whole person'). It has to broaden experience and prove its worth by providing a sense of enjoyment in learning. All educational institutions, therefore, make provision for this wider concept of student welfare. All will, for example, have sports facilities, encouraging everyone to keep fit and healthy. For the real sports enthusiast, many will be able to arrange specialist training, providing access to professional coaches for those particularly adept at their sport, for example. If you don't want to be a player, you may well enjoy watching sport – and the UK, of course, has many students amongst its notoriously passionate sports fans. Many institutions will also have facilities for other interests, such as music, art or drama. Those with a talent in these fields will be encouraged to cultivate it – though there is no pressure on anyone to do so. Many institutions have 'writers in residence' or 'artists in residence', established professionals who are willing to give their time to encourage you to learn from their example. The purpose of all this is, of course, partly to allow you to develop a range of skills and interests outside your immediate academic subject interest. But it is also linked to a belief that study is best achieved when students feel comfortable and relaxed. What are called 'extramural' interests (meaning interests developed outside the lecture room) can often make a large contribution to your sense of personal satisfaction.

Youth culture

There are a whole variety of different ways in which you can relax. Britain has a vibrant youth culture, in cafes, clubs and pubs, with a music and entertainment scene well known – particularly to those in the relevant age group – by many people from outside the UK. And as a student, you are very much part of it. Clubbing and music have a big appeal for many. Films, plays, concerts, TV and radio are just as popular. This interest in entertainment may serve as a refreshing distraction from studies but it can also shade into another aspect of study. Students in the

UK customarily meet together in societies, to debate, to discuss, to keep each other amused, to enjoy old interests or to cultivate new ones. Every institution will have its student social life, its societies, groups and clubs. These groups may have a programme linked to academic studies. Some invite visiting speakers. Even the most distinguished visitor is pleased to have an invitation to speak to students. Being part of this student culture helps to develop other aspects of your personality, to provide you with a wider outlook on the world. And it also makes it easier to make friends, to join group activities, to take on a leadership role, if you are so inclined, or simply to participate. Most students would argue, however, that the primary function of any student social group is to allow everyone to have fun. The rest is an incidental bonus.

EMPLOYMENT PROSPECTS

Many students feel that their main motive in studying in higher education is to improve their job prospects. You undertake your studies to get on to the first rung of your chosen profession. There is indeed unequivocal evidence that a university education does help you to get desirable employment and also helps you to advance more quickly in your chosen career. But, when first embarking on university studies, most students are not committed to one particular job. You look to university to offer a different kind of employment advantage: it equips you with what is usually called transferable skills. Amongst those skills which are currently in high demand with employers and which the British higher education system is often said to emphasise are:

1. self-motivation (being able to work independently and with commitment)
2. time-management (being able to decide on priorities and to finish tasks promptly)
3. working under pressure (being familiar with the need to balance competing demands)

4. meeting deadlines (being able to work within time-constraints)

5. team-work (being familiar with working in groups and being able to play as a team member)

6. cultural awareness and breadth of interest (being active in wider studies and extramural activities).

SOME QUESTIONS

Choosing the UK, then, also means choosing a form of education with definite or particular characteristics. These will appeal more to some students than others. Even for British students, there is a leap to be made from school education to undergraduate education and from undergraduate to **postgraduate** studies. The pace of learning quickens, the breadth of knowledge covered widens and the element of conceptualisation grows. For international students the change can be even more marked if the initial education is in a different language or involves a different style of learning. Of course, university **lecturers** understand these differences and an effort is made to integrate everyone at the start. But if you are contemplating study in the UK, first ask yourself: what will be familiar and what less familiar to you? What rewards would you expect to gain from studying in the UK? Do the benefits which studying there will bring outweigh the effort which will be necessary to obtain them? Is the challenge of a different educational system something you feel relaxed about and would welcome?

2 CHOOSING AN INSTITUTION

THE CHOICE

If you decide to choose the UK, it is then necessary to select a particular institution or a small number of institutions from which your final choice of study destination can be made. There are quite a number to choose from. In the higher education sector, there are almost 250 different universities and colleges, some new, some old, some large, some small, some general, some specialist. There are even larger numbers if you include **further education** colleges, many of which award degrees. And there are also specialist institutions of a great many different kinds. Given the number of colleges and universities and the range of courses on offer, how is this choice best made? Again it becomes necessary first to think about your personal situation, to decide what you are looking for and what you most and least enjoy, and then to seek to match your personal needs to what is on offer. There are a range of factors which may be relevant to a choice of where to study – the reputation of the institution, its location, the precise course which you are looking for and the fit between your qualifications and the institution's requirements.

Reputation

Students often decide to choose an institution by its reputation, and there is obvious sense in this. By studying at a prestigious institution, you share in that prestige. Employers are likely to take it as a sign of your ability and ambition. It can open doors. But there are other considerations here which need to be kept in mind. The reputation of any institution is not a static matter. Reputations can last over long periods, but they do sometimes rise and fall. You also need to be aware that all the evidence available about an institution is historical (that is, it relates to a reputation already won). Those searching for a place are most likely to want to know that that reputation will be sustained into the future (even into a time beyond graduation when you are looking for a job). It is therefore necessary to obtain the latest information and to interpret it with care. Reputations are also sometimes partial: some institutions are held in very high regard for some aspects of their work but not for other aspects. Sometimes institutions themselves talk about their 'centres of excellence', meaning areas in which they can claim some distinction. But this equally implies that there are areas in the same institution which do not enjoy an equally high reputation. Moreover, a centre of excellence for one institution may be an average department in another. It is necessary to know a little about the source of the reputation. If the source is one person, as is often the case with league tables compiled for newspapers, or if it comes from the institution itself, it clearly lacks the force of something produced by or with the backing of some public body.

League tables

League tables, though always of major interest to students, are a particular problem since it is often difficult or troublesome to find out on what criteria they are based. Some of these criteria may be important for you, others utterly irrelevant. Nowadays there are so many league tables that they seem almost to cancel each other out. Individual institutions quote whichever table they feel can be presented in a way favourable to them. Moreover, the final placing is usually the result of an average mark, deduced from a number of variables. In many cases the average is likely to be misleading. For example, if an institution has two main subject interests, in one of which it is held to be excellent and in the other mediocre, the mark assigned will be an average one. But that mark is a just indication of the quality of neither of the subjects under review. You really need to be confident that the table you are examining is reliable and valuable and that it is dealing with subjects which you regard as significant. And you need to look at a number of different indicators of quality in order to satisfy yourself that the reputation is soundly based and (to use a favourite word in **academia**) robust.

Quality audits

Recognising some of these problems, the British government has set up a system of quality inspection of teaching and research to which all institutions are subject and which all must recognise. This was a real advance for those trying to get a guarantee of quality. But it has also been extremely controversial. The massive amount of bureaucracy involved in compiling the information required for the surveys has led institutions almost to the point of rebellion. With each successive revision, the government has sought to allow for a less burdensome quality control mechanism. The danger, of course, is that the distinctions then become less marked. And even government-backed, professionally enforced systems of inspection are all going to be subject to the problems already discussed: they will be historical, partial and to some degree subjective. They will also be influenced by government policy, which in the UK has been not simply to record difference but to foster and reward innovation and experiment (which may not be your main consideration). None the less, in being the first to introduce a system of peer review (assessment carried out by experts from other institutions), and in working to ensure that that review is more practical and refined, the UK government has made quality inspection an accepted part of higher education. Even if the system is changed in future in response to continuing criticisms of its operation, some kind of assessment scheme of value is likely to remain. Currently the two principal tests of quality used are the Research Assessment Exercises (RAEs) and the Teaching Quality Assessments

(TQAs). These are published and are available on the Internet and all institutions will be able to provide you with an indication of their results.

One final problem with assessments is that they must all seek to standardise results in order to be intelligible. But the infinite variety of courses, subject divisions and approaches to study do not make this an easy matter. Even a subject as widely understood as history can appear in many different forms: as political history within politics; as economic history within economics; as social history within sociology; as ecclesiastical history within divinity; as constitutional history within law, and so on. Those who assess different programmes have to decide on the parameters of their investigation. In doing this, they may push different departments with different reputations and outlooks within a single category of investigation or divide those who regard themselves as forming one coherent entity. This, too, can make the final assessment a puzzle rather than a clear indication from which conclusions can be freely drawn. To make matters worse, over time different methods of presenting the results have been employed by different boards, and particularly between the Scottish and the other assessment systems. None the less, quality assessment is a guarantee of minimum standards within an institution. It is worth taking into account on that basis. It also helps to overcome the problem that some institutions are so new that they have not yet had time to build up a popular reputation. That may not mean that they lack quality. Treated with appropriate caution, the official assessments can be a really helpful guide.

FINDING A COURSE

All the research on why students choose particular institutions emphasises the importance of the particular course. Undergraduate students and 'taught' postgraduates generally search first for a subject and this then leads them on to a series of course titles. But a knowledge of subject and title is seldom enough. They then have to know the course content, and it is generally on this basis that the choice is made. The content of the course indicates not only the topics being covered but also the approach being taken to the subject and the ideas which lie behind that approach. This will differ in virtually every institution. Each is responsible for its own degrees and each decides how that degree will be composed. Which themes are included and which excluded, which approaches utilised and which disregarded is a matter which every institution has to decide for itself. All this makes for a great range of choice even within a single subject. For undergraduates, there is the further possibility of specialising in not just one but two subjects (often called 'single' and 'combined honours degrees'). As different course combinations are available at different institutions, this extends the range of degrees on offer even more widely. It is also possible to take a general (or non-specialised) degree which offers the widest choice of all.

Course listings

How is it possible to find out the contents of any course? Some of the various bodies responsible for giving generic information, like the British Council or appointed educational agencies, may be able to provide you with lists of the institutions which offer courses in a particular discipline. And the search can be continued from there. There are also lists of course offerings for individual institutions on the Internet. If these have not been recently revised, they are not certain to be complete or entirely up-to-date and will probably again need to be checked. Courses change at bewildering rates: academic staff move on; new approaches are introduced; older ones are discarded. It is wise to search quite widely, too, since the same subject can be taught under a very large number of different subject headings, let alone course titles, in different institutions. Biology, for example, can appear under biology but also under biological science, life sciences, biochemistry, biotechnology, developmental biology, ecology, molecular biology, plant science, genetics and zoology, to name but a few. But any list, even an abbreviated or out-of-date one, will form a starting point. It is also possible that, rather than starting with just a subject interest, your choice will already have been narrowed down to particular institutions or particular regions. If so, it then becomes necessary to know only how to set about obtaining the specific information which each institution can provide about itself, since this allows you access to a great deal of information on the contents of its courses.

Postgraduate research programmes

For research students, where there is seldom a course as such, the choice is generally much simpler. Postgraduates are likely to be attracted to an institution by knowing the work of one of the scholars or one of the research groups based there. Of course, scholars are mobile and you need to check that your information about their location is up-to-date. It is also important to establish that the institution which interests you has an established reputation in your research field. Without this, it is unlikely to have the research materials you will require or to be able to provide you with the fullest support and back-up. Research is increasingly inter-disciplinary these days. It is worth establishing not only what the staff and resources are to assist with supervision in your immediate field but also what is available in allied areas of study. If you can, it is wise to obtain from the institution an account of the research which its research students have conducted in your area in the immediate past in order to check that the approaches and the topics seem relevant or attractive to you. If you can also correspond with a current or recent student and gain a first-hand impression, it is even better. For an intending research student, expert advice, good facilities, a congenial environment and a proven track record of success are usually the main considerations.

The prospectus

Every university or college will provide everyone on request with a prospectus. These are generally annual or bi-annual publications. They sometimes include all the courses at all levels within that institution. More commonly, there are separate prospectuses for undergraduate, postgraduate and part-course or occasional studies. To obtain the necessary information, it is important to specify which is required. Quite commonly today, prospectuses are available on the Internet and can be read there, and later a hard copy can be sent for, as should certainly be done once your serious interest has been aroused. A prospectus gives a great deal of information. This will include general information about the institution (its situation, its reputation and its facilities amongst these), information about all the study opportunities available and instructions on how to apply. Not a few will also include information about costs, about funding, about accommodation and about student social life. Generally, prospectuses are written with domestic students primarily in mind, but there is often a section for international students or instructions on how international students can enquire further. Undergraduate prospectuses and prospectuses on taught postgraduate programmes will generally describe the course in some detail, providing precisely the kinds of information about course content which students find most valuable. Postgraduate research prospectuses will list the research work going on in each unit and will also indicate any particular concentrations of activity or currently active projects. In many areas of study, they are likely to offer some details on the research facilities and equipment available, too.

The university web-site

In addition to the prospectuses, all universities now have their own web-sites. These usually give access to a huge amount of information from the general to the specific. Individual departmental information is often available and this can include materials which are much more extensive than those in the prospectuses (though that is not yet something on which you can always rely). You can generally also find lists on the web of the academic staff and often of their research publications or current research activities. One problem with the web is that, unlike the prospectus, it does not always bear a date. You need to have information that will apply to the course at the date when you will begin your studies. It is wise, therefore, not to rely on the web-site alone. On the other hand, the immediacy of the Internet may mean that the information given there is in fact the most up-to-date available, surpassing even that in the prospectus, which takes months to assemble, print and then issue. Since, as already observed, courses do alter, academic staff change and facilities improve, it is wise to get the latest information available. In the end, if any doubts remain, it may be necessary to write directly to the institution to check that the information you have is currently valid. All prospectuses and web-sites usually supply postal and e-mail addresses to enable enquirers to do precisely that.

CHOOSING A LOCATION: TOWN AND CAMPUS

Where is the best place to study? Colleges and universities in the UK are found in virtually every geographical environment and in most parts of the country. There is again a need to consider options. The principal distinction, at least according to the college prospectuses, is that between a city-centre institution and a campus one. These are, however, very broad categorisations and not necessarily mutually exclusive. As one form of analysing differences, they can be helpful. But, if you are intending to make location a key element in your choice, you may need to ask many supplementary questions.

The archetype of a campus university is a small academic community set apart physically from urban life. The campus is often pictured as surrounded by its own walls and forming a little self-contained unit. It is often presented as a haven of peace, set apart from the hurly-burly of modern life, with an atmosphere which encourages scholars to think and students to study. By contrast, a city-centre university typically occupies property either grouped together or dispersed amongst other public and private buildings in the middle of a city. The university's activities are thought of as forming a part, however distinctive and specialised, of urban life. Its staff and its students are engaged in academic work but are also viewed as involved in city life and caught up in all its excitements. In fact, these descriptions are closer to caricatures than archetypes. No university campus is as entirely isolated and no city-centre university is as totally submerged as this suggests. But if the contrast is often exaggerated, it is widely deployed and you need to be aware of it.

Campus life appeals most to students who want a relatively cloistered life. The campus is a means of separating out some college activities from other aspects of daily life and providing a concentrated sense of academic community. This can be liberating and relaxing for some, claustrophobic and precious for others. Often campus universities, within their own grounds, are places closer to nature, looking out onto rural landscapes. This can be appealing, relaxing and conducive to study, but some find the isolation unwelcome or even inconvenient. City centre universities are much more part of urban life, though normally they have principal buildings, usually grouped together, where the academic community is concentrated. Within these, too, an attempt is often made to provide most of the facilities which students need. Being in a city can mean for some greater choice and variety and for others a less evident sense of community. Students in city-centre institutions will feel part of the institution but will also feel part of the city. For some this can be exciting, lively and a stimulus to study, for others it can be anonymous and overwhelming. City-centre universities are generally preferred by those who actively seek involvement in the wider society and who enjoy or at least respond to the pressures of urban life.

The contrast between campuses and city-centre institutions is often overdrawn mainly because both types have elements in common with the other. In any case, if most of the university clearly falls in one category rather than another, particular departments or divisions may well be cited elsewhere and the alternative category may fit them better. There are also many universities and colleges in towns and smaller cities where neither the city centre nor the campus model quite applies. They, too, will assert the benefits of their particular location, arguing that their students feel more of a significant part of the local community, not submerged in cities or isolated on campuses.

Metropolis and regions

Some students choose a location by selecting a place they already know or where they have connections. Most students will be aware of the principal cities in the UK, particularly London, the capital. This knowledge in itself is likely to (and indeed does) provide a great appeal. The political and cultural life of London especially is known and recognised all over the world. London is also likely to be the place where the largest communities of expatriates from other countries will have formed, and these can be an important social support for some individuals. But London is also one of the largest cities in the world, the largest by far in the UK, and the most crowded in which to live. This can give it glamour and allure but can also make for inconvenience, particularly in travel, and for a greater sense of pressure on those who live there. Since most of the other major cities have an active cultural life, with, many would argue, rather less pressure and inconvenience, they are often held to offer equally enticing prospects.

Communications

Sometimes distance from the capital is another factor which students consider, though it may not always deserve the attention it attracts. Ease of communication is usually as important as distance. The UK is a relatively small, compact and homogenous society. Distance is not a tyranny as it can be in other countries. Travel into and out of the UK and between its major centres is relatively easy and need not be expensive. Most international airlines now make extensive use of regional as well as London airports, giving more choice when deciding on routes and fares. It is possible to fly to most of the regional centres in the UK directly from many European capitals and sometimes directly from cities further afield. Quite often, airlines with UK domestic partners or which fly into UK airports tend to discount the price of onward travel from their hub or home-base airports. Britain also has a reliable internal transport system (though a national peculiarity of the UK is to pretend otherwise), which reaches every city and town in the country. To travel from London in the south of the country to Aberdeen in the north is only just over an hour by plane, seven hours by train and twelve hours by bus. Intervening points are generally likely to have correspondingly more rapid and equal ease of communication.

Local living costs

Local cost of living is another factor which students often consider. The urban centre is usually more expensive for accommodation than suburbia or rural areas, though it can be cheaper for other necessities, such as study materials. There are also some clear differences between different regions. London, particularly, and the south-east of England, more broadly, is regarded as the most expensive area in the UK. As a generalisation, it is probably true to suggest that costs then fall in the rest of the country in proportion to the distance from London. In Scotland, the main cities of Edinburgh and Glasgow, which like London are metropolitan cultural centres with a wide appeal to outsiders, are, however, though distinctly cheaper than London, rather more expensive than their distance from London might suggest. Most universities give estimates of local living costs in their prospectuses. These are obviously a helpful guide. But it would be unwise to use them comparatively. They are quite often offered as an aspect of recruitment and there are striking differences in what the figures contain and in how they have been compiled. Some are almost the minimum required for survival; others are averages calculated on the basis of a fairly comfortable lifestyle. In any case, cost is partly a matter of the quality of service. For nearly everyone cost is important, but most people feel a balance needs to be struck between cost and things like facilities, convenience, comfort and interest.

The weather

Weather is another factor often mentioned as a concern by potential students. Britain is a country in which the four seasons are an evident part of an annual cycle. Some people dislike seasons and prefer a perpetual summer – a view, however, little supported amongst those from countries which do experience very long hot, humid, sultry summers. Britain, being a small country in the temperate zone, offers in fact only relatively small variations in climate, temperature or rainfall throughout the year. It is not uncommon to see snow in the winter or to experience some nights when the temperature falls below zero degrees Celsius. Summer temperatures rising into the high twenties Celsius are also encountered. But extremes of heat or cold are very rare. There is also relatively little variation throughout the whole country. Though the average temperatures in the north and in the uplands of the UK are lower than for the south and the coast, the temperature variation is not marked north to south or east to west. Britain is largely an island and it is this which gives the weather its most characteristic features. All areas are subject to quite unexpected and sometimes unpredictable changes, so that the changing weather is one of the favourite subjects of social conversation in the UK. Commenting on the weather is in fact still one of the ways in which British people greet each other. For those who need to know the statistics and who want to know which areas are the warmest, the coolest, the wettest, the driest, these too are published, often broken down by city or region. But it is wise also to find figures for your own country, area or city with which to compare those for the UK. Our assumptions about our own climate are often wrong.

The four seasons do have a further consequence on which students often comment. There is real variation – particularly marked in the north – between the hours of daylight in summer and in winter. In the height of summer in Scotland, daylight can last for up to eighteen hours per day; and in the very depth of winter this can be reduced to eight hours per day. Most people unused to such differences find the seasonal variations interesting and enjoy the transition from principally outdoor to principally indoor entertainments (and then back again), which is a feature of the changing seasons. But this can sometimes mean waking up when it is still dark during one season or falling asleep when it is still light during another, something initially strange, except perhaps to the nocturnal. Fortunately, students seem to adapt to it, as they do to differences in temperature or weather conditions, quite instinctively.

SOME QUESTIONS

Choosing a college or university again involves looking at a range of features. Which ones do you regard as important and which unimportant? Given your preferences, which institutions would you want to include on your shortlist? How will you decide which will suit you best of all? (Remember that your list will have to be fairly tentative at this stage, however, as there are further factors to be considered, of which the likelihood of obtaining a place is clearly amongst the most vital.)

3 GETTING THE REQUIRED QUALIFICATIONS

UNDERGRADUATE ENTRY

There are three elements to qualifying for university entry as an undergraduate in the UK. The first is to have obtained a qualification that is 'recognised' (that is, accepted as a sufficient academic test to allow you to be considered for entry) by your chosen institutions. The second is to have achieved a standard in that qualification which is likely to win you a place in competition with others who are applying to the same institution. The third is to have included in your qualification examination passes in particular subjects, if any are specifically required for the degree at which you are aiming.

Standard and non-standard qualifications

If you are applying for entry as an undergraduate from outside the UK and you have British qualifications or internationally recognised 'standard' qualifications (like A levels or the International Baccalaureate or American SATs), then there is clearly very little doubt that an application can be made straight away. But when your qualifications are 'non-standard' (in other words when they apply to one country's educational system and are not normally used as entry qualifications by other countries) then knowing whether or not they are sufficient for entry to a particular UK institution can be more complicated. There is no rule about it. One institution in the UK may accept a qualification which another university rejects. Acceptance could be because the university feels the qualification has special relevance for its courses or it may simply have greater experience, by having admitted many students with that qualification in the past, in knowing how to use it to set reliable entry standards.

There are, however, common conventions which most institutions observe. For example, when the local qualifications bear a close relationship to UK ones, such as those of many Commonwealth countries in East and South-east Asia, recognition is almost always given, even though the examination systems are different. If there is no close relationship, of course, recognition becomes much harder to predict. But it is not ruled out. The best way to check is to look up the prospectus. Many prospectuses provide a list of the national qualifications which are recognised for entry purposes. If yours is not on the list or if there is no list, you should enquire directly.

Entry levels

The level of performance (the scores or grades or results achieved in your university-entry examinations) forms the second element in the requirements. In most cases, the UK institution will expect not just a simple pass but a performance at a particular standard above a pass. Usually, the particular level required is also set out in the prospectuses, using British school grades or standard international grades. The required level is likely to be different for different degrees and for different subjects within the same degree. If your qualification uses a grading system which bears a close resemblance to the 'standard' ones, it may be possible for you to see whether or not you have a real prospect of getting admitted. You may even already know your grades and so be able to deduce whether or not you have reached the required scores. Needless to say, when your results are as high or higher than the specified level, you can be certain that you have a very serious prospect of winning a place. If, however, you find it impossible to say what level in your 'home' qualification is the equivalent of the level required for British students, you may once again have to write and enquire. You could also, of course, simply decide to apply. Once you do so, the university will tell you if your qualifications are sufficient or what standard in them you must still achieve.

Subject requirements

The third requirement is that your university-entry qualification must often include certain subjects which relate to the particular degree for which you are applying. For example, if you want to study languages, you are likely to have to include a foreign language in your list of qualifications. If you are studying science, it is likely that scientific subjects or mathematics will feature, and if you are planning to do medicine, chemistry or biology may well be required. If you hold no examination passes in the required subjects, you may find that you must spend some extra time acquiring them or you may have to change your choice of degree. Once more, these requirements are generally set out in the prospectus, using UK and international examinations. If you are unclear what the equivalents would be using your own qualification, you will again have to enquire directly. But if you decide to apply, the problem will once more disappear, as you will then be told specifically what subjects you need to pass and at what level.

Access courses

When your qualification is not 'recognised', the university which you have approached may recommend that you should take a preparation programme, usually called an 'access' or 'foundation' course. The reason why recognition has not been given is often because of differences between your university entrance qualification and UK entrance qualifications in content, standards or length of studies. An access or foundation course or other preliminary programme is used to supply what you are judged to lack.

Doing an access course usually means spending one school

year studying in the UK. A few access courses are tailor-made for particular groups of students and can take less time, but that is not the norm. UK access and foundation courses in most cases blend some English language skills improvement (where that is required) with advanced courses in a number of school subjects (such as economics or chemistry or geography) chosen to match those required for entry to different UK degrees. You will get advice on what to choose from the institution to which you are applying. In some cases, even when you do have 'recognised' qualifications, you are still asked to take an access course. If your qualifications lack some of the specific subjects required for the degree course you want to take, for example, again you may be recommended to follow the access route.

Access courses are available in the UK in schools, further education colleges and universities. To apply for entry, what you require normally is your school-leaving certificate and perhaps a letter of recommendation. If you are not a native speaker, you will also need evidence of your proficiency in English (some programmes can take absolute beginners in English, but they are very much fewer in number). A few access programmes are also offered outside the UK (though not in every country by any means). There is also sometimes an alternative route to the same end. In some countries where pupils take the 'non-standard' national qualification, it is also possible to sit for A levels or the International Baccalaureate or SATs at a local school or college. This, however, is not always easy. It may even require you to opt out of the national system altogether. Your school teachers will know and should be able to guide you.

Open and tied access programmes

Some access courses also provide you with what is in effect a conversion programme. They prepare you to sit the final university entrance examinations of the UK (either A levels or, in Scotland, Highers) or standard international university entrance examinations (like the International Baccalaureate or SATs). These examinations are also 'recognised' outside the UK, so access courses can be your means of qualifying for university entry in other countries, too. Not all UK access courses, however, are of this type. Others have examinations unique to one programme. These non-standard examinations are not automatically recognised as equivalent to university-entrance examinations by all UK institutions, still less international ones. Only the colleges and universities associated with the particular foundation course are bound to accept them for that purpose. If you choose a place on one of the programmes which has its own examinations, therefore, you must find out in advance whether the university or college in which you are proposing to take your degree is associated with that particular access programme. If it is not, you must ensure that it is at least prepared to allow you to count the course to complete the qualifications you require.

Access courses also differ in the content of the programme and the choice of subjects offered. Many are bolted on to university or college courses, forming what is sometimes called year zero, so that entry to the first year of the degree programme is guaranteed to anyone performing satisfactorily. To get on to those tied access courses, you first have to apply to the university or college concerned, using your local qualifications. If you already possess most of what it requires for entry (but lack some elements), it will then recommend or require the access course as a supplement. By passing the access course, you complete the required qualifications. But you may then be under an obligation to remain with the university making the original offer. Programmes which prepare you to sit UK national or international qualifications are not generally attached to any specific university degree course and so leave your choice of institution open. In those cases, however, there may not be a guarantee of entry to a particular institution at the end of the access programme. All will depend on how well you do in your examinations and how closely your exam performance matches the entrance requirements of the institutions to which you have applied.

Access through further education

For those in need of extra qualifications to enter undergraduate study, the further education system in the UK offers an alternative route. The UK has made serious efforts to integrate its various educational qualifications into a single scale. Those who leave school at 16 and subsequently enter employment and gain vocational skills often then discover an interest in returning to full-time higher education studies. For them, a route is available into universities which involves obtaining qualifications within a further education college. The principal awards are General National Vocational Qualifications and their Scottish equivalents, the Scottish Vocational Qualifications. The GNVQ and SVQ structures can lead ultimately to the award of a Higher National Certificate and Higher National Diploma. Both these awards can give access to university study. Where the fit with the university studies is close and the standard attained high, HNDs can even provide advanced-level entry. In England, Wales and Northern Ireland this can be entry into second year and in Scotland into third year of undergraduate study (though the exact exemption is a matter for the university to determine).

The Higher National Diploma route is designed for those with less specific academic qualifications than A levels or the International Baccalaureate. Since it also emphasises breadth rather than depth of study, it has sometimes been regarded as particularly suitable for those international students whose school education has been similarly broad in coverage. In some respects, it can also be easier to enter and to access. Though sometimes used for university entry, however, the main purpose of HNC/HND courses is to provide qualifications with a vocational relevance. They are intended chiefly to show that their holders have reached a particular vocational standard and so can take on extra responsibilities at work. That kind of qualification, however, is also valued by many international students.

TRANSFERS

Some students who have begun a degree at a university outside the UK are permitted to transfer and complete their degree at a British university. Generally, this requires some strong reason for why you wish to transfer. For example, if your parents have moved to the UK to work and want the family kept together, you may be considered eligible. Those who transfer are often allowed to count work done at their previous university towards the award of their UK degree. But this depends on whether there is a match between the subjects studied, the level of difficulty and the content of the courses. Usually, the student has to take extra time and to study extra subjects in order to be allowed to transfer. There are, however, a few cases where some British universities have arranged with universities abroad to take students on transfer without requiring extra work. This is often called a 'split degree programme' and normally operates only when course schedules and examination systems have been carefully co-ordinated between the sending and receiving institutions.

POSTGRADUATE ENTRY

To qualify as a postgraduate, what you need is a bachelor degree from a recognised university. This is sometimes further defined as a degree 'at honours level'. The class of honours may also be specified (usually it is 'an upper second' or a first 'class honours' degree). Most universities in the world are, in fact, recognised in the UK, and you can usually expect that your degree will be acceptable (though degrees from more prestigious places are likely to appeal more to admissions officers than those from less prestigious ones). If in your earlier degree studies you concentrated on the subject which you want to study as a postgraduate, it is also likely that your degree will be regarded as equivalent to a UK honours degree. The only problems which you are likely to meet are when the period of your undergraduate studies is shorter than in the UK or the content of the degree is very different.

Deciding on the grade equivalence of a British 'honours' degree, however, is not so simple. If you are in any doubt, you could consult UK NARIC (the National Academic Recognition Information Centre for the UK), a body which gives advice on the equivalence between UK qualifications and qualifications worldwide. Its web-site is www.naric.org.uk. No institution, however, is obliged to take the advice which UK NARIC provides. You could also write to your chosen institution, setting out your results and asking if these will suffice. But there is a difficulty with that, too. Every applicant in the UK is considered individually and life-skills and professional qualifications can weigh along with academic ones. The institution, therefore, may suggest that you should first apply, so that the entire range of your qualifications can then be considered.

Postgraduate degrees: subject requirements

In general, your bachelor degree has to correspond to the postgraduate programme for which you want to apply. Some international students suppose that anyone with a bachelor degree in any subject can decide to move to an entirely different subject when applying for postgraduate studies. For example, science graduates sometimes enquire about taking a postgraduate degree in English literature and business studies or psychology graduates will enquire about chemistry. Though there have been exceptions for people of outstanding ability, such complete changes of discipline are, for most practical purposes, impossible in the UK. A very few postgraduate courses do specify that they are open to students with a degree in any discipline. A few more are designed to allow you to convert your studies from one discipline to another. But in general you will be expected to continue with the same subject in which you specialised as an undergraduate or one nearly allied to this. If you have decided that you dislike the subject you specialised in as an undergraduate and that you now want to change, you can apply to take a second undergraduate degree. In some cases, you can then be granted exemption from some of the requirements for this 'second first degree' (as it is sometimes called) and you may be able to graduate sooner than students taking an undergraduate degree for the first time. But that is a matter for the university to decide, after looking at your qualifications.

Postgraduate access

It is rare for postgraduate programmes in the UK to require foundation or access courses. Direct access for those with a bachelor degree from a recognised university is the norm. But a number of such courses are available. Some of these are largely English language improvement courses, with study skills and study of some specialist subject included. A few are aimed at converting other less well known national qualifications into ones regarded as equivalent to British bachelor degrees. Others provide some top-up elements to knowledge required for specific entrance purposes. Amongst the most popular in the field are access or foundation courses for the Master of Business Administration (MBA). They closely resemble courses offered by some continuing education or lifelong learning departments in being aimed at those who already have a degree but whose study skills, after a period in employment, are rusty. Most MBA courses, however, do not require an access programme, though they do usually expect applicants to have a bachelor degree (normally in any subject, not just in business).

ENGLISH LANGUAGE QUALIFICATIONS

In addition to entry qualifications which are 'recognised' and examination results which seem to provide you with a good chance of winning a place, you may need proof of your English language skills. If English is not your native tongue or if most of your school education has been conducted in another language, you have to present some evidence of your ability in English. Several English language tests are normally acceptable, including IELTS (International English Language Testing System) and TOEFL (Test of English as a Foreign Language). Generally, IELTS is the preferred test in the UK. You must check the requirements with the universities where you hope to apply. Many students apply even before they have taken a test or before their current English score is sufficient. Sometimes you are obliged to do that in order to meet application deadlines. But the universities can then make only a conditional offer; you have to get the required result before they can issue you with a final offer. What you are asked to achieve is a minimum score. Many students feel that to reach the minimum is not enough and so undertake further studies before they start their course. This is certainly a good policy. Weakness in English is notoriously a major cause of academic difficulty for many international students.

Where should you do your English studies? Some people think that it is best to take a course in the UK. A great many such courses are available. Courses last from a few weeks up to a year or more. You can choose from those which offer basic language improvement to those dealing with specialist forms of English (like legal or business or medical English). Many of these courses are accredited by national bodies, like BASELT (British Association of State English Language Teaching) and BALEAP (British Association of Lecturers in English for Academic Purposes), which gives them a quality guarantee. The advantages of studying English in the UK are that you are then immersed in an anglophone culture. You use the language continually in your daily life and hear the precise forms which will be of most use to you in your studies. While you are studying, you can often gain some insight into teaching and learning methods in UK institutions, too. This is especially true if you take a course in English for Academic Purposes – something widely available in the UK. Obviously the quality of instruction is also likely to be high.

But there are other considerations, too. Studying English in the UK may be more expensive than studying it at home. You will have living costs as well as fee costs. The course will probably demand your attention full-time. That may make it difficult to work or to do other studies at the same time. Some students feel that they cannot afford the time or the costs involved. But, if that is your decision, a short period of study of a few weeks just before commencing studies is widely recommended and widely adopted. It gives you time to adjust to your new environment and helps you to become used to the local variants in English. When you already have a high EFL score, however, even a short period of English preparation may not be necessary.

SOME QUESTIONS

Which of your qualifications seem likely to be of most help to you in applying to study in the UK? How will you decide whether it is necessary or desirable to undertake further course preparation?

4 ENQUIRING AND DECIDING ON A COURSE

INITIAL ENQUIRIES

At some point you need to narrow down the range of course choice considerably. Once you have obtained prospectuses and your needs and interests are clearer, it ought to be possible to do this. You may then feel you have enough information for you to decide which institution you prefer and which course you want to take. If you are still uncertain, it is advisable to correspond with some of the universities or colleges which appeal most to you. You can get in touch with them by email and letter. Anything which remains in doubt can then be clarified. The universities usually have an international division with a desk officer or counsellor who will be familiar with international students' needs and will be able to deal with any matters relating to the whole institution. The desk officer will also be able to forward letters to a department or even to an individual member of staff if the question requires a very specific response. Given that letters are likely to arrive from many different correspondents, however, it is important to be as precise as possible with any questions. Stating clearly your level of study (undergraduate or postgraduate), the intended subject of study and the nature of the qualifications which you hold will ensure a more precise answer and reduce the time taken to obtain it. Remember also to check that the information sought is not already clearly available in the prospectus or on the web, for example. But asking questions will not threaten your chances of being accepted or expose your academic weaknesses. You are free to write and to write repeatedly until you are satisfied that you have all the information you need in order to make a decision on whether or not to apply.

UNDERGRADUATE DEGREES: THE PROFESSIONAL COURSES

If you are intending to study as an undergraduate but are still uncertain about what you want to study, you need to think about what you intend to do once you graduate. Some students are interested mainly in professional degrees (like medicine, architecture or accountancy). Almost all of those who take these degrees intend to pursue a career in the discipline. Since many of these courses are also very popular, you have to be aware that you are unlikely to win a place on them unless you are strongly motivated to join the profession. Those who choose a professional degree have usually been attracted to the profession for some time. Many will already have gained some experience of it or will at least have taken some active steps to find out as much as they can about it. Medical students, for example, will often have done voluntary work in hospitals or surgeries or will have undertaken charitable work in support of the sick or the elderly. Veterinary medicine students will have gained experience of looking after animals. Architecture students may have built up a portfolio of artistic work and have shown skills in mathematics (their buildings have to stand up as well as to look attractive to the public). Engineers will have shown a practical interest in technology. Media students will have done some related work, such as serving on the school magazine or taking part in the school play or working in amateur radio. The university selectors for professional degrees often say that they are as much interested in your personal profile (that is, in your character, outlook and interests) as in your school qualifications (though those are clearly important, too).

Choosing to follow a profession at a young age does require some maturity. In some countries, these degrees are open only to graduates. In the UK, they also demand high and specific entry requirements. As a result, those who apply for professional degree places have often been taking subjects at school with precisely this goal in mind. This commitment is in fact often the key to their success. Yet, like all other university degrees, professional studies can also be regarded as an intellectual training. A few students do complete them and then follow other career paths after graduation. Usually, there are also recognised escape routes available for those who decide at an earlier stage that they would prefer not to enter the profession. Medical students can sometimes turn to science, for example, or architecture or accountancy students to social sciences. Being often the longest of the UK undergraduate degrees, professional degrees can also require rare financial as well as personal investment. The careers to which they lead on are undoubtedly amongst the most sought-after in the modern world. But it would be very unwise to embark on professional studies without appreciating the commitment which they demand. And it is infinitely better to have considered alternatives before commencing these degrees rather than trying to find the best escape route out of them afterwards.

UNDERGRADUATE DEGREES: ACADEMIC COURSES

Most undergraduate students choose degrees which are not specifically linked to a profession but have a broader base, such as those in the humanities, sciences or social science. These degrees are particularly suitable for those who have clear academic preferences but do not yet have a very definite idea of the employment they would prefer. The attraction is usually to study something of intellectual interest while keeping job options open. University selectors for these degrees will generally be looking at your aptitude, intention and interest. They will assess your aptitude by examining how well you have performed at school in the subject areas of relevance to your choice of degree. Usually, the relevant subjects are obvious though it is wise to check in the prospectus. For business studies, for example, a knowledge of mathematics is often required and for some social sciences it may be English. To test your intention, they will want to discover why the subject interests you now and what you hope to do after you graduate. Most prospectuses will guide you on which areas of employment graduates have chosen after entering any particular degree. To have some general career plans in mind, even if only to avoid closing off some options, will help you to determine your choice and will help the selectors to know that you have given the choice some thought. Finally, interest is important because university studies do require motivation and stamina and the selectors will want to be assured that you will not give up easily.

Apart from 'general' degrees, in which breadth of study is emphasised, most 'intellectual training' degrees are taken as 'honours' programmes, in which you specialise in one ('single' honours) or two ('**joint**' or 'combined' honours) particular disciplines. These degrees provide you with both a specific disciplinary focus and general transferable skills which open up prospects in many different vocational areas. The choice of discipline may be important for your career plans; often, it is not. Almost all degrees, for example, are thought to be of value for those contemplating working in some fields of government service or of industry or commerce. Providing you get your degree, most employers in these fields will tell you that they are less interested in exactly which academic subject you have studied than in what your studies have meant for you. If you feel enthusiastic and confident about what you have studied when you graduate, you will be highly desirable as an employee. If you emerge from your studies looking as though you have been through the mangle backwards, you won't be.

Thinking ahead a little is one way of deciding which degrees would make a good choice for you. For example, if by choosing a combined or general degree you feel you are gaining something of value in your studies and opening up attractive prospects for your future employment, they may be worth considering. But if you feel they would distract you from what is your main subject interest, they may not. What you are looking for is something which seems to contain the right elements for you, that fits with your interests and plans, that carries your studies forward and gives evidence of being accessible, achievable and worthy. The UK offers a very wide choice of single honours subjects and different combinations of subjects within joint honours. Many of these disciplines will be new to you, since they are not taught in schools. Many of those which are taught in schools are presented at university in a rather different way, which will make them seem unfamiliar. Choosing precisely which degree programme to apply for is, therefore, not always easy and you may wish to make yourself as fully informed as possible about them before making your decision.

POSTGRADUATE DEGREES

The two principal postgraduate degrees in the UK are the master's and the doctorate. Master's degreees are generally of two forms: one-year programmes and two-year programmes. The master's is often described as an intermediate degree, meaning that it is taken by some students as a step towards achieving the highest of the academic awards, the doctoral degree. But in more recent years the master's has become very much a self-standing degree, often taken to secure professional qualifications or to enhance vocational prospects. The one-year 'intensive' master's is one of the UK's most popular degrees amongst international students. It lasts twelve months, rather than the normal **academic year** programme of nine months, and is usually strictly time-limited, so that all the work must be completed within the period prescribed. It is therefore a testing programme and most students find it very hard work. The two-year master's is quite similar in form to the doctoral degree and is often taken by those aiming at a career in academia. There are also a number of **diploma** programmes, some of which are shorter versions of one-year master's. In most cases, however, the diploma is not a separate degree in the UK but is a stage on the way to the completion of a one-year master's. Usually there are examinations to mark the end of the 'taught' phase of the programme (often after nine months) and before the research project begins. Those who pass these exams are sometimes awarded a diploma and may leave at that point. But those who do sufficiently well (generally the bulk of the **class**) go on to undertake the project, at the end of which (if they are successful) they are awarded the master's degree.

Postgraduate courses

In the UK postgraduate degrees are generally of four types. The most common is advanced studies in a subject in which you have already specialised in your undergraduate degree. The second is a conversion course in which your undergraduate specialisation is converted into a specialisation in an allied field, one which has normally been a minor element in the earlier degree. Chemical engineers, for example, can sometimes take a postgraduate course to become chemistry specialists, human biologists to become psychologists, or sociologists to become social anthropologists. The third type is a professional degree in which the academic knowledge gained from undergraduate study is turned into a specifically vocational purpose. Examples include courses which law students take to train as lawyers, accountancy students take to train as accountants, or social science students take to train as social workers. The fourth is an 'experiential' course, where students are mainly reflecting on and theorising about work which they have carried out in employment rather than undertaking further work in their undergraduate specialisation. Examples of experiential courses include the MBA (Master of Business Administration) and advanced social work degrees. These are often open to those with a bachelor degree in any subject (or in a wide range of subjects), but they usually also require a minimum of two or three years of appropriate work experience. There are, however, exceptions. The UK has a number of MBA courses, for example, which are not based on students' work experience but are business management courses open to anyone with undergraduate qualifications in that area of studies.

Postgraduate taught courses and research courses

Postgraduate degrees often distinguish between taught and research programmes. Students sometimes find this puzzling and ask which would be better for them. There is even a suspicion that one or the other imposes extra demands, linguistically or academically, on international students. In fact, taught and research courses have some elements in common. Both are likely to involve attending some lectures and tutorials and carrying out independent project work. Clearly, however, the balance varies between the two, the research degree involving more independent work and the taught degree more lecture attendance. Amongst one-year master's courses, the lecture or taught degree is the more common, even in courses which are designed to provide you with the background to conduct research, such as in many MRes (Master of Research) degrees (which are also normally one-year programmes). But there are also some which are primarily research programmes.

Many international students say they prefer one-year courses with a large taught element, simply because this makes the course seem more structured, with the steps to be achieved (completing essays and examinations) more clearly demarcated along the way. But research programmes have work demands and deadlines too (and you can request even more, if you want). There is certainly an extra excitement to research work, which some students appreciate, and many enjoy the feeling of working at an educational frontier, discovering new things for themselves, rather than mainly studying what is already known. With taught programmes there is little danger of the programme extending beyond the minimum period and that is a major consideration for some students. But taught courses do require you to perform well from the very beginning. Research programmes give you a little more opportunity to find your feet before the **assessment** starts.

Recently, a number of UK universities have introduced a doctoral degree with a distinct 'taught' component. This was produced partly in response to a request from international funding agencies which felt that research degrees were more valuable when students were also provided with a grounding in a number of allied subjects. These degrees tend to take longer than the traditional research degree in order to accommodate the taught element. But they usefully blend the more structured approach of taught degrees with the freer approach of research degrees and so are held to have an academic as well as vocational or practical appeal. They can perhaps be seen to mark the culmination of a longer development in the UK, which has increasingly seen a fusion of 'taught' and 'research' elements in postgraduate degrees.

ENQUIRY CONTACT POINTS

There are several ways in which you can get an overview of all the degrees and courses that are available in the UK. One way is to visit your nearest British Council office. These have been set up in most countries in the world, some within British embassies. They serve a variety of purposes. One central goal is to give advice to those looking to study in the UK. The Council offices also often provide information through websites (many of them will even be able to provide access points), literature and desk advice. Attached to a number of these offices is a specialist advisory service, for which financial support comes both from the Council and from the British higher education institutions, namely Education UK (formerly called the ECS, Education Counselling Service). Its officers are expected to undertake promotional work on behalf of UK institutions and they are also expected to provide advice for enquirers. British Council offices, however, are not uniform across the entire globe. Some are large, some small, some have specialist educational staff, some don't. Each is likely to offer a range of services. Most of these services are free but for others a charge may be made. You should contact your local office, explain your interest and enquire about what is available.

As a UK agency, the British Council is not there to give impartial advice on whether to study in one country or another: its advice relates to the UK only. But on education in the UK, it is usually able to dispense advice without fear or favour. The only exception to this is where the Council has contracted with a British institution to provide a programme which it wishes to offer wholly or partly in-country. This applies, for example, to the British Council English-language schools and to a number of other courses, such as some MBAs, delivered in part by distance-learning methods and in part within Council offices. These are often excellent, but one would not expect the local staff to be asked to choose between them and similar courses available in the UK.

Exhibitions and fairs

In many countries, Education UK and a number of public and private educational bodies arrange education fairs or exhibitions to provide information about study in the UK. These events are often widely advertised in the local press, on university web-sites and by the British Council. They are sometimes held in big exhibition halls, sometimes in schools or colleges. Representatives from a large number of UK institutions, each with its own stand, are available there to meet you (and your parents and friends and advisers) personally. Usually, they bring with them from the UK prospectuses or subject leaflets. Their intention is to be able to offer you individual advice and assistance. If the exhibition is crowded and they cannot answer all your questions immediately, they will provide contact details and then correspond with you. There is usually a stand there representing the UK in general at which you can enquire, even if the institution which interests you most is not present. Sometimes these education fairs include representatives from institutions in other countries as well as from the UK. The fairs do tend to be very busy and individual counselling time is quite limited. If you go, it is wise to note down your questions beforehand so that you can get them answered promptly.

Agents

Another method of getting helpful information is to consult a local agency which is known to provide reliable advice. British Council offices can often put enquirers in touch with local commercial educational agencies. These exist in most countries and almost all of them advertise widely in the local press. Sometimes they give advice freely (by making a charge instead on the universities or colleges when they subsequently admit the client), sometimes on payment of a fee by the enquirer, sometimes both. In some countries these private agencies have earned a very high reputation for knowledge, probity and efficiency. In some cases, they are very closely linked to particular UK institutions and can provide up-to-date information about their partner institutions and an insightful application service. In a number of countries there are 'approved' or 'accredited' lists of agents, which provide some safeguards about the service provision, and sometimes these lists will have been endorsed by UK authorities, too.

None of this, however, provides a full guarantee of quality service. Even in countries where agents have to be licensed and inspected, it is wise to check further. Word of mouth is the usual recommended means by which agents are approached, once it has been ascertained that the agency is 'recognised' and of good repute. It is always worth exploring how long the agency has been in business and what familiarity it has with the educational system of the UK (such as counsellors who hold British degrees). If you have a particular institution in the UK in mind when considering the approach, it is only sensible to ask that institution whether it has any knowledge of or connection with the agent. Agents will, of course, wish to direct their clients towards those countries and those institutions with which they have business contacts, which may not be the best suited for your purpose. It is therefore important for you to have done your research and to be prepared to tell the agent exactly what you require. None the less, like the British Council, agents may well be able to provide a great deal of skilled and impartial information about the UK, its educational system and the courses available for anyone considering studying there.

The Internet

You can also seek advice either by writing to the UK or by using the Internet. There are now a very large number of websites which can be used to gain access to information about UK higher education. The most highly recommended is again that of the British Council. Recently a new British Council web-site operated through Hotcourses.com and with marketing support from Yahoo has been instituted, which incorporates and may finally replace its earlier ones. There are also quite a number of web-sites within the private sector. Many of these are comprehensive but you should be aware that they are all, like the Hotcourses one, funded in part by their subscribers. This may mean that a particular institution is less well served by them since it has chosen not to subscribe or to subscribe only minimally. It may be a sensible rule that while general information can be relied upon, particular information needs to be treated with greater care or used only to gain access to an individual institutional web-site.

Friendly advice

All the evidence suggests that students don't make up their minds to study abroad just by what they read or by what they have been told by agents or advisers alone, however reliable their sources. They usually turn to friends, to teachers, to sponsors, to those they know who have lived in the UK and who know something of its ways. This is clearly a sensible thing to do. The information obtained through such contacts may not be expert at assessing educational excellence (though this is usually easy to appreciate and judge). But it is highly personal, it often comes from those with an awareness of your individual circumstances and it offers a point of view which is likely to resemble your own very closely. Friendly advice from informed compatriots, therefore, is a source of information of great value. You should certainly take every opportunity to avail yourself of it.

Many universities have country-based alumni organisations. If there is one where you live for the university which interests you, you should be able to obtain the name and address of the secretary by enquiring directly. Even when no formal organisation exists, the university may be able to send on your letter to a local alumnus or alumna who is willing to answer questions about the institution. Particularly when you have no personal contacts, these former students are often the best available source of free and expert information and advice. It is often said that a satisfied customer is the best advertisement for any product. In the same way, an enthusiastic graduate is likely to convince you more quickly than any other source of information. Equally, a dissatisfied former student is usually able to give a powerful critique which will make you keenly aware of the pitfalls and of what you need to do to avoid them.

SOME QUESTIONS

What sources of advice on study in the UK are open to you at home and how do you propose to find out about others? In deciding which course you will study, what do you think makes for 'a good course'? Many people now use the Internet to discover information about study in the UK. What information can you derive in that way and what will you need to find by other means?

5 APPLYING AND GETTING ACCEPTED

ENTRANCE REQUIREMENTS

In making an application for a study place in the UK, you obviously have to be confident that your qualifications match the requirements of the institutions to which you intend to apply. One feature of the British system is that there is usually no common entrance standard for all degree programmes even within a single university. Different subject areas are likely to have different requirements, reflecting the number of places available, the popularity of the programme and the skills held to be necessary for the course. Sometimes a combination of requirements is demanded: general academic attainments, judged by your overall result, and specific skills requirements, judged by your knowledge of particular subjects. You also need to realise that the requirements given in the prospectuses are there purely as a guide, an indication of what has been sufficient to gain entry in the past. Even if you have attained these, you cannot be absolutely certain that you will receive an offer of entry. But it is then very likely.

Most institutions will publish in advance the standards they require for entry to their various degree programmes. These will vary significantly not only within institutions but between them. The most prestigious programmes are likely to have very high academic entry standards, though this partly depends on the number of places they have to offer as well as the demand for those which they face. Other programmes will have more modest academic requirements, perhaps because of relatively low demand or because of a greater provision of places. Some institutions will also want to keep their academic entry standards relatively low in order to attract more candidates with other qualities (such as those of character or experience) which the course is held also to require. There is therefore likely to be a wide range between the most and the least demanding.

Matching qualifications and places

To guard against any uncertainty, most students usually have more than one institution in mind when thinking of applying. For undergraduates, the centralised admissions service in the UK (UCAS) actually allows you to apply to up to six places simultaneously. Obviously it is not necessary to do this. It is still possible to apply for only one or two places if you prefer. Finding a place at any level is not simple: places are limited. Each degree course can take on only a relatively small number of students at a time. The whole system is, fundamentally, competitive: each applicant is trying to win a place against others who feel that they are also worthy of admission. Generally this means that when more students apply for a course than before, the qualifications required for entry will rise; and when fewer show any interest, they will fall. When applying, you are therefore aiming at a moving target and cannot be quite certain that you have hit it until you are allocated a place. Whatever your own qualifications, it is clearly important, therefore, that you make your application as powerful and effective as possible to give you the best chance of success.

APPLYING AS AN UNDERGRADUATE: UCAS

There are different application systems in the UK for undergraduates and postgraduates. In general, undergraduates apply through a centralised admissions service known as UCAS (the Universities and Colleges Admissions Service). You have to obtain the UCAS form, complete it in good time and follow all the instructions about when and how to submit it. Remember, too, that the deadlines for applying to Oxford and Cambridge universities and for applying for medicine and veterinary medicine are earlier than for other places and subjects. The forms are generally available at British Council offices and can be obtained by writing directly, and an electronic form is available on the Internet (www.ucas.ac.uk), or via email: app.req@ucas.ac.uk.

The UCAS system can enable you to keep your options open. With just one application, you can apply to up to six institutions simultaneously. It also allows you then to select on the basis of offers you receive. But the system involves a detailed application form and can initially appear quite cumbersome and bureaucratic. Its merit is that usually it is at least not too difficult to follow, and your school counsellor is likely to be able to advise should any difficulties arise. When first making an application, it is important that a lot of thought is given to the UCAS form. If you change your mind about what you want to do once you've made an application, it can become quite complicated to try and sort it all out.

A few UK institutions permit or require direct application outside UCAS and will, after admission, inform UCAS of their decisions in order for a full UK record to be kept. But to apply directly will generally deny you the opportunity of being considered by any other British institution. Those choosing to apply other than through UCAS, therefore, have to be confident that the institution expecting direct application is your clear preference and that you stand a good chance of meeting all its conditions when you apply.

The UCAS form requires you to give an account of what you have studied and what marks or grades you have obtained at school. You have to apply in good time, often up to nearly a year before you actually commence your studies. International students are usually allowed to apply later than 'home' students but you have to check. Applying well in advance, often before you have even sat your entry examinations, means that sometimes you have to give predicted rather than actual results.

The application also requires other documents which have to be prepared for the purpose. In place of letters of recommendation, which feature in most application systems, the

UCAS form requires a report on each applicant from someone in authority in school. Schools are given instructions on what to include in these reports. The essential point to note is that this is an occasion for comments to be made not only about the pupil's academic record but also about other factors which point to the prospects of success. There is an opportunity here for the school to discuss potential, to compare and contrast one pupil's achievements against those of others and to provide a rounded portrait. The school report is the counterpart to the applicant's personal statement, which the form also requires. This personal statement is an opportunity for you, as the applicant, to demonstrate aptitude, motivation and commitment, and it needs to be written so as to bring out those features. Admissions officers are often required to choose between candidates with similar qualifications and two matters can then be of real importance in the final selection. One is the impression which you have conveyed to your teachers of your ability, character and potential (on which the teachers provide an opinion in the institutional report). The other is the impression that your personal statement conveys directly.

The 'asking price'

Some undergraduate advisers suggest that you should apply to the institutions with the highest 'asking price' (i.e. academic requirements) which you are likely to reach. Others suggest that you should hedge your bets, by applying to places with a variety of different entry requirements. If you feel that the high 'asking price' also reflects your own perception of the desirability of winning a place in that institution, then you ought certainly to consider applying. But an asking price is simply another kind of league placing, a measure produced by the combined effects of the number of places which the institution can accommodate weighed against the number of students applying there for entry. This may not always be a true indication of the best for you. It is better to use the asking price alongside other indications of desirability in making your decision about the choice of institution or course. But if you judge the place an attractive one and you meet or expect to meet the necessary requirements, there are, of course, strong arguments in favour of trying to win a prestigious place. Then the academic ability of the students and the rigour of the course will push you to achieve your best.

Getting accepted as an undergraduate

If you are applying for a place as an undergraduate and you hold standard international qualifications, like the International Baccalaureate, or if you are taking a recognised foundation or access course, the selectors will be able to make a decision on your application quite straightforwardly. For everyone else, the main concern for the selectors will be how to interpret school results from countries outside the UK. In some cases, this will be the predicted results, as you will have had to apply before the results of your final school-leaving examinations are known in order to meet the deadlines. Most UK universities have a specialist office or an individual empowered to make offers of places. The interpretation of results, however, is seldom automatic. No two qualification systems are identical in what they measure and, as already mentioned, all applicants to UK universities are considered individually. The UK institutions will also want their selectors to use their judgement in order to find the best candidates. They will want them to consider personal factors like motivation and maturity as well as academic ones. Selectors will, therefore, look at the qualifications which you are offering and will try to see how far these match what the institution sees as necessary for success. The institution's needs will vary according to subject or area of studies and may even vary according to the date of entry for which you are applying. The selector's job is to find the best candidates, meaning those with the highest and most appropriate qualifications and – what may not be the same – those who seem to have the greatest likelihood of success, amongst all the applications received. That is why motivation, character and experience as well as grades and results can be given weight.

If when you apply you have already taken your university entrance examinations and the results are known, the selector can offer you a place unconditionally or your application can be rejected outright. More commonly, your results are not yet known and selectors are obliged, if they want to offer you a place, to make it a condition that you must achieve specific grades in your examinations. As a result, it is not unusual for those applying to six institutions to find that they receive a variety of different responses, some unconditional offers, some conditional offers (meaning that results still have to be obtained before the offer is confirmed) and some rejections. You then have to decide what to do in the light of the offers you have received. You are asked to make a first choice and a reserve choice by a closing date, based on your offers. If your first choice is an unconditional offer, the place is yours. If it is a conditional offer and you subsequently meet the condition, again you are smiling. If, however, your preference is for an offer held conditionally and you then fail to meet the condition, the institution is not obliged to admit you (though you have the right to appeal).

Clearing

There is also a special procedure within UCAS for undergraduate applicants who have applied but who have not managed to find a place by the closing date. The same procedure is also used by students who apply too late. It is called 'clearing'. It tries to link up the courses which still have vacancies at the end of the application period with the students still looking for a place. The courses with places still available are published on the Internet and in UK newspapers. Clearing requires students first to identify those courses and those institutions which interest them and then to approach the institutions concerned and negotiate with them directly. This is, of course, a backstop measure but it does enable everyone to be more flexible about choices in order to be successful in finding a place.

APPLYING AS A POSTGRADUATE

For intending postgraduates, some of the same issues can arise as for undergraduates. For example, you too may find that the entry requirements given in the prospectuses relate to UK and international qualifications rather than to those you hold. As already mentioned, postgraduate applicants are often asked to have 'a bachelor degree at an honours level from a recognised university'. What do you do if you hold a degree which does not have the title bachelor or uses a grading system that doesn't use the term honours? Usually, there is no problem. Admissions officers are extremely experienced. They are aware that the titles of university qualifications differ and they usually know or can rapidly discover what their institution would regard as equivalent to UK degrees in any other educational system. If any doubt exists, it is probably because they have to examine each student's qualifications individually. The admission officers may decide, therefore, that though one element in your qualifications is not sufficient for their purposes, other elements could compensate for this. Particularly, if you have not yet obtained your final results when you make your application, the selectors may ask you for more information to enable them to make up their minds.

Postgraduates have to apply directly to the institution or institutions of their choice and not through some central admissions service like UCAS. Usually postgraduates are more certain than undergraduates about where they want to study and why, but they too need to be accepted. The application forms are available directly from the institution and can sometimes be found at the institution's web-site on the Internet. It is possible to apply to any number of institutions at the same time. Generally there is no cost involved, beyond the time and effort required to complete the forms, although applying widely might be better kept reasonably confidential as it could be held to indicate uncertain commitment. The application form will make it clear if any application charge is levied but this is rare. Generally, postgraduate application requires three essential pieces of information to be included with the form. Firstly, you will be asked for a transcript (an official statement or record, supplied by the university which awarded your undergraduate degree and any subsequent degrees). Secondly, you will need references or letters of recommendation or at least the names and addresses of two or more referees. And finally, you will have to send proof of your English language competence in terms of a recognised test score, such as IELTS or TOEFL.

Postgraduate applications: transcripts

You have yourself to obtain a transcript from any universities in which you have previously studied; and the transcripts are normally required in English. An undergraduate transcript usually gives an account of all the courses studied for the undergraduate degree qualification and of the mark or grade obtained in each, as well as providing an assessment of overall performance. A master's degree transcript is likely to be briefer but again may contain some information about the content of the programme as well as about the overall result. If the university from which you graduated cannot provide a transcript in English, a copy of the original could be sent, together with an authorised translation. The transcript is used by the admitting institution to assess how strong you are academically. It is also used to check that you have the knowledge required for the course for which you are applying. And it may be used to provide evidence about individual interests and enthusiasms (sometimes suggested by the fact that you have done particularly well in some aspects of the studies but badly in others, for example). If you have postgraduate certificates or diplomas or advanced degrees other than a master's, transcripts or copies of those should also be included since they add to the attractiveness of your candidature and provide more solid evidence upon which the selectors can rely.

Postgraduate applications: references

One of the major requirements for all postgraduate applications is the letter of recommendation or what is usually called the 'reference'. Normally applicants are expected to give university teachers as their referees, since they are held to know your previous work well and also to be able to judge accurately your future academic potential. If you have a feeling that your teachers don't know you well enough to do that, other references can be included with a request that the university might consider them. Sometimes 'character' referees (people who can vouch for your personal qualities) or 'work' referees (people who have supervised or observed you at work) are also required. Most universities want confidential letters of recommendation, that is letters which you have not been allowed to see. It is hoped that the referee will be frank and open with the receiving university about all your strengths and weaknesses in a way which might not be possible if you were to see what was said. For this reason, many universities insist on conducting a direct correspondence with the referees in which you play no part, other than having provided on the application form your referees' names and addresses. But in other cases you may be asked to obtain the references, perhaps sealed and signed across the seal of the envelope, for you to send on along with the application. Slowness in obtaining references or transcripts when the correspondence is undertaken directly by the institution can delay the work of deciding on an application. It sometimes speeds things up if you can check with your referees – as courteously as you can – that they have received a request to send the reference and that the reference has in fact been sent.

Timing your English language test

To take an English language test requires advance planning. The two principal tests of English worldwide are the US test called TOEFL and the UK/Australian test called IELTS. There are test centres in many countries where these can be taken at dates which are widely advertised in the local press. You must check which English tests are acceptable to your institution and when these can be taken. Universities set their own English language levels, so the scores you will be expected to obtain are likely to differ between institutions. There is usually also a difference in the requirement for language-based disciplines and science-based disciplines, the former requiring significantly higher scores. There may be a difference as well between undergraduate and postgraduate requirements. It is important that you should have the result in good time. If you have applied for a place before you have taken the test or before the result is known, you will be eligible only for a conditional offer. But in order to arrange the immigration formalities of entry into the UK as a student you need not a conditional but a final letter of admission. You therefore cannot afford to delay taking the test too long. Immigration formalities, of course, also require time to complete.

Other postgraduate assets

Where this is relevant, some institutions will also want to know about your work experience, publications and contribution to society. The intention here is to build up a more rounded picture of you as a candidate, your interests, skills and outlook. Postgraduate work is often isolating and demanding and the institution will want to know not simply that you have the academic ability to be able to pursue the course but also the stamina, commitment and conviction to see it through to a successful conclusion. This can sometimes be deduced from other evidence and so may not be formally required. You should not feel that you will be disqualified if you have not been in employment, or have not published or have not made what you suspect is meant by a relevant contribution to society, unless any of these is specifically mentioned as a key entry requirement for the course.

Applying for research degrees

Doctoral research students are often asked for an additional – and important – extra requirement. You are told to prepare 'a research proposal', meaning an outline of the research which you propose to undertake. This has to indicate clearly the field in which you wish to work and should give some idea about a topic which you think might be worth investigating. The closer you get to defining a precise project the better. If you have enough background to indicate exactly the subject on which you wish to work, this should certainly be specified. But it is recognised that intending research students cannot be fully aware of all the research that is proceeding at the time of their application. A statement on your principal interests and an indication of why these interests were aroused may be enough initially. In order to avoid duplication with other research projects, to ensure that the project can be completed in the time available and to match your interests to those of the supervisors, some redefining or refining of the topic after commencing studies is quite normal. As an intending postgraduate research student, you are also free to write directly to your chosen institution and to correspond with your particular department. Indeed, a direct correspondence about what you want to study before you apply is probably the best way to ensure that the institution shares your interests and that your application is likely to be well received when it is finally made.

Assessing postgraduate applications

One difficulty for postgraduate admissions officers is that of judging from your application exactly how able a student you are. They, of course, will have a clear idea of what they are looking for and will search your transcript and references for evidence. They may know of other students who have applied from your country, perhaps even from your institution, and they may have a sharp insight into what they are expecting as a result. But, if you feel there is likely to be any doubt, it still makes sense to give as much information as possible in your letter of application about the quality of the degree you have obtained. One way of doing this is to ask your referees to say in their letters how they would rate your performance against those of others from your institution who have applied in the recent past to undertake similar postgraduate work elsewhere. You yourself may be able to give your class placing. This gives the selectors another yardstick by which to measure your performance.

Professional postgraduate studies

In some countries, it is the postgraduate degree, particularly in vocational fields such as medicine, law, architecture and engineering, which trains you to enter a profession. The undergraduate degree is seen as a period of foundation studies, a general academic training in liberal arts or sciences. This is not the case in the UK where such professional degrees are available at the undergraduate level. But there are also postgraduate degrees in professional subjects available in the UK, and some may be open on a 'conversion course' basis to those who studied other subjects as undergraduates. These, however, will generally not be suitable for those seeking professional accreditation, though they will have an importance for those working in careers ancillary to the profession. For example, a postgraduate law course may well be open to someone with a humanities or social science degree. This will not provide a qualification to enter the legal profession but will have relevance to those wishing to pursue careers in business, journalism or in government service. If you do want to practice law, then you will normally have to take a law degree as an undergraduate followed by a professional legal training course. Some students who have taken a law degree, of course, may also then take a postgraduate law degree, too, particularly those wishing to enter the academic world or one of the other professions mentioned. The same considerations apply to many degrees in public health or in professions ancillary to medicine.

Postgraduate medical degrees often create a particular area of confusion. Most postgraduate medical degrees (with the exception of those in the ancillary areas and in public health) are science-based studies. They allow students to do work which deals primarily with the scientific basis of medicine, though the studies they undertake may also contribute eventually to better clinical practice. Clinical courses in the UK, however, are normally provided not by the universities but by the Royal Colleges of Medicine, of which there are a number covering everything from surgery to psychiatry. These are often linked to training programmes within the UK National Health Service and they often employ university teachers to do some of the instruction. But, when teaching on these courses, the lecturers are then wearing a second hat, as employees of the Royal College rather than of the university. Those in search of clinical training, therefore, are best advised first to approach the General Medical Council, which oversees the work of the Royal Colleges. If a course is available linked to university studies, the GMC will be able to provide details about it (www.gmc-uk.org).

Application deadlines

For postgraduates, the number of places available is likely to be quite limited. If places are filled on a rolling basis, this will make the time of application extremely important. The earlier the application is made in the academic year, the more likely it is to be accepted. One possible exception is that of research degrees, where vacancies may occur at times other than the start of the academic year. But that is not certain. Many research students have to undertake a generic training before they begin the research element in the degree, and this is usually offered only once, at the beginning of the year. That may rule out starting dates at other points in the year. In order to be considered in time, it is possible to apply and it is sometimes even necessary to apply before you have obtained the qualification on which your entry will be judged. Admission to UK institutions generally has a long lead-in time, quite often of six months or more, with a specified date by which applications must be submitted. On or before that date, the selectors will offer places to all suitable candidates. If there are still vacant places after that date, they will usually be prepared to consider 'late' applications; but they may decide not to do so and may ask all others to wait until the following year. For research places, the pressure can be greater still. Few supervisors can take more than five or six research students at any one time. Even if the applicants are supremely well qualified and the selectors strongly favour the application, there may be no place available. It is always wise to follow the institution's instructions on deadlines. Most starting dates are likely to be fixed and not negotiable.

SOME QUESTIONS

Making an application for a place in a UK university is not difficult. But it does require thought. How have you decided what the selectors are likely to want to know? What educational background do you think they are looking for from you and what personal qualities do you think they will expect? Bearing this in mind, how should the application form be completed so as to maximise your chances of success? Finding out something about the university, the department and the course to which you are applying will be part of this process.

Will you be able to indicate that you know something about
the institution and the course for which you intend to apply?
Where will you be able to show you have given some thought
to the relevance of this study for your future? If you've done
both, it is much more likely that you will convince the selectors
that you are worthy of admission.

6 STUDY ABROAD PROGRAMMES

WHAT IS STUDY ABROAD?

Study abroad is one of the earliest forms of international education in the UK. It has grown in popularity and now exists under a very large number of different names, study abroad, junior year abroad, year/semester/term overseas, occasional study, visiting study, non-graduating study and (in its European Union variants) Erasmus and Socrates, amongst others. Study abroad is a programme for students undertaking studies leading to a degree in a country outside the UK who wish to spend some time studying in a British institution as part of that degree. While in the UK, the students take classes and thereby usually gain 'credit' (in other words, they complete the course work and examinations and are assigned an overall grade for their efforts). This credit is then transferred back home and counted towards the award of their domestic degree. Almost all UK universities welcome students applying on a study abroad basis. A great many colleges and universities have signed agreements with partners in other countries to foster and support this form of study. Though most of these arrangements are with institutions in North America and the European Union, universities from many other areas, including Australasia, Eastern Europe and Japan, also participate.

Study abroad programmes chiefly exist for undergraduates though a small number are available for postgraduates too. Their primary characteristic is that they offer students from one country an opportunity to gain an experience of study in another country by participating in classes alongside local students. By being undertaken in a country with a different culture and by requiring close contact with that country's students, study abroad is certain to expand your personal horizons. It can also expand your academic horizons, too. Usually you have an opportunity to take courses which are not offered at your home institution. Some study abroad students, for example, select courses with a British or European focus. Some are able to find courses in areas of their main subject not covered at home or which are presented in the UK in an unfamiliar way. A number move into new areas, choosing perhaps subjects which are available solely or primarily in the UK or in which the UK institution they have selected enjoys a high reputation. Others follow exactly the programme they might have taken at home, but find the different teaching and learning styles of the UK to be their principal interest and challenge. All of them, whatever their course of studies, gain a new perspective on their own education by being able to compare it with the one they come to know in the UK.

CREDIT TRANSFER

For most students, credit transfer is at the heart of study abroad. Normally credit is given both for the period of study undertaken and for the level of attainment (meaning the overall mark or grade) achieved. As a result, students who gain 'full credit' can complete their degree in the same length of time as those who remain throughout at their home institution. The study abroad and the study at home then become precisely analogous. This, however, does usually require that the subjects taught in the two institutions match and that similar academic standards prevail in both, which is why the opportunity is often restricted to particular institutional partnerships. It also requires that the university calendars should run on compatible lines. The British academic year generally runs from September or October to May or June. If your university year runs on another annual cycle, such as from January to December, participation in study abroad may inevitably involve some extension of the study time or may require some special arrangements or compromises.

In some cases, the arrangement for credit transfer is automatic, having been agreed in advance, often in a document signed by both the sending and receiving universities. It can also be part of an international structure like the Erasmus programme. You can discover whether any such arrangements exist and what their terms are simply by enquiring at your own institution. In general, to obtain credit, you will be expected to select appropriate courses, attend classes and do all the work (tutorials, laboratory work, essays, examinations) which your British counterparts in the same class are doing. Particularly if you find that the studies are open only to students from one department or area of studies, a prior agreement with specific requirements of this kind on the credit terms is to be expected. In many cases, however, there will be no agreement. You may find, none the less, that your university has a policy of encouraging (or at least permitting) its students to spend a period abroad and that it is willing to give you credit for the work you perform there. If that is the case, you will probably be expected to apply independently to the British institution of your choice and you will be required to follow the rules which apply to all other students there. That means you will have to take the same number of courses and to do the same amount of assessed work. And that may well be different from what you are used to at home. It may mean that three courses in the UK have to take the place of five courses at home (or vice versa) and that marks given in one scale will have to be re-calculated in another before they can be assigned to you at home. But all decisions on credit transfer, on what you must study and how you will be assessed, are primarily a matter for your home university.

ENQUIRING

Your first port of call in applying for study abroad has to be within your own institution and particularly its Study Abroad or International Office or whatever other name the agency bears. It is there that you will discover if there are agreements already in place which specify the UK universities to which you can apply and which provide details on the terms under which you can obtain credit. If there are no partnerships of this kind, it is there that you can ascertain whether study abroad is still permitted and, if so, on what basis. Where partnerships exist, you will normally be expected to apply to the UK institution through your home university and it will have all the application forms and prospectuses or study guides that you will need. If there are no partnerships but you are free to apply anywhere, the UK universities can be approached directly and they will send you their forms and prospectuses or tell you where to obtain them on the Internet. Some universities in the USA ask you to apply through an intermediary agency which specialises in arranging study abroad programmes. You have to contact the agency and it will guide you further. If you don't know where to begin, try getting in touch with the International Office at the university where you would like to study in the UK, expressing your interest and asking for information.

CREDIT EQUIVALENTS

Deciding what credit to give to the studies you perform abroad when the course arrangements and marking systems are different can be difficult for everyone concerned. The European Union has tried to deal with this problem by setting up its own system for credit transfer, called the ECTS, the European Credit Transfer System. Those assigned with the task of devising this system rapidly discovered that the sheer diversity of structures and assessment methods which prevailed within the EU required them to operate on the basis not of mathematical precision but of mutual trust. What one country considers a completed educational programme, for example, is now recognised by all partners as such, even when there are marked differences in the composition of similar programmes in the two partner countries. Assessment methods, which can vary enormously, are a particular concern and guidelines have been established for 'translating' one system of marks or grades into another. Some universities both within and outside the EU have devised their own solution to the assessment problem by setting out in advance for their students how the studies and grades obtained in the UK will be translated when credit is assigned at home. Where this has been done, you obviously need to know about it. In the USA, the intermediate agencies which are sometimes used not only devise methods for standardising the interpretation of the work performed and the assessments obtained but also oversee the recruitment and placing of the students in UK institutions. Obviously anyone planning to study abroad will want to know about whichever credit transfer arrangement is in operation and to be fully aware of the requirements before embarking on any programme.

APPLYING FOR STUDY ABROAD

Many UK universities publish a guide to their study abroad programmes. When available, this is extremely helpful in explaining procedures. Guides generally set out course choices. Having investigated where and what you can study and having decided that the study matches your needs, you can use them to make your course selection. To apply for a study abroad place in a UK institution, you will probably have to submit a transcript, an account of your degree progress to date, the courses you have taken and the passes and grades obtained. You are also likely to need a couple of references from your university teachers, as the host university will require some evidence of your ability to cope personally as well as academically. Many study abroad application forms specify that you will need 'ambassadorial qualities'. The reason is that you are likely when abroad to be seen as a representative of your institution, perhaps even of your country, and the selectors will want to be assured that you are going to leave a good impression on your hosts. If you are coming from a university where English is not the language of instruction, you will also have to submit an IELTS or TOEFL or other English language score. Course selection for study abroad can be more complicated than for domestic students. You may find that you have to correspond with your host institution if there is some doubt about how far you meet the requirements for entry to particular courses or if you have the opportunity to select from a number of options. But generally the paperwork involved in applying for study abroad is less onerous than for full-degree study.

EXCHANGES

Many study abroad programmes are technically exchanges. For each student from your institution who goes to study at an institution in the UK, another comes from that institution to yours to take his or her place. This tends to put a limit on the numbers who can participate, even though the balance of flow is not always exact. But there may be some advantages in this. Since one of the purposes of study abroad is to experience a different university system and to gain an understanding of a different society, many students expect numbers to be limited to ensure that the experience is kept authentically 'British'. Limited numbers, however, mean competition. If study abroad is arranged only through an exchange, you may therefore require a strong academic record to be accepted. In most cases, in fact, particularly where procedures and agreements are already in place, as with the Erasmus and Socrates programmes, the first hurdle is to be selected by your own university.

FEE ISSUES

Reciprocal exchange programmes and those arranged on a university-to-university basis often involve fee-waivers. You may still be liable for fees at your own institution, but you will not usually have to pay fees at the host one. Many study abroad programmes are what is sometimes called 'one-way exchanges', meaning that though credit transfer arrangements are in operation, no student needs to move in the opposite direction for a place to be made available. Such one-way exchanges almost invariably involve fee payment to the host institution (though you may be exempted from paying to your home university as well or it may collect your fee and then reimburse the host university on your behalf). On the other hand, more places may well be available on one-way programmes than on reciprocal exchanges and they are often more open in terms of subjects or areas of study. To participate in these one-way programmes, of course, you will still have to get permission to apply from your own institution.

KEEPING IN TOUCH

If you are required to apply to the UK directly yourself and there is no intermediate organisation to which you wish to turn, you will be expected to keep your home university informed about what you are studying and what results you have achieved. But where your university strongly encourages study abroad on a one-way basis it usually has an office to help you make the application and to arrange the credit. If you are hoping to transfer your credit, you will also have to agree with your home institution, once the host university offers you a place, the exact programme of studies you propose to undertake. You will usually be expected to take courses which fit with your home curriculum. Should any changes in your course selection take place subsequently, particularly once you arrive in the UK, you will also have to get approval for that. This means maintaining a close contact with your home institution and you should have established how to do this and noted down e-mail and other contact details before departure. The same applies to reciprocally exchanged students, who may also be involved in late course changes.

STUDY ABROAD AND EFL

If English is not your first language, you may be able to take a study abroad programme combined with a course in English as a foreign language (EFL). Usually, what you do is to take the EFL course first, perhaps for a few months, to boost your English language skills. Then you join in with the students doing undergraduate degree classes. Sometimes your English is good enough by then for you to drop further EFL study. Sometimes you continue with EFL and take the undergraduate courses in addition. These combined EFL/study abroad programmes do mean that students whose English-level is below the normal undergraduate entry point can still apply to participate. Of course, the EFL part of the programme involves studying alongside other international students in separate classes, not alongside local students. But in the study abroad classes, you do join in with the other students. There are usually some limitations on the study abroad classes you can take, however, especially if you are going to stay only for part of the year. There can also be difficulties in allowing you credit for these classes if you do not complete a full-course programme. These joint courses in language and study abroad can also sometimes be more expensive than study abroad programmes on their own. But they are still popular. Students often gain a lot in confidence from them both in their use of English and in their familiarity with British undergraduate life.

SELECTING COURSES

Course selection for study abroad students can be complex. There can be major differences in the courses which students take in their first few years at university in Britain and in universities abroad. These differences can even extend to studies in school. First year courses in UK universities sometimes require a previous knowledge of the subject gained at school. This may make even introductory university courses in some disciplines less accessible to you (though there is often an alternative course for complete beginners). In the UK, university study tends to be progressive. In other words, the second level of a course usually demands knowledge of what has been covered in the first year and the third level may require a knowledge of both first and second year courses. If you come from a different university background, with different structures, different lengths of courses and different contents, fitting into the UK system may require some flexibility on your part or on the part of the host institution. And learning to operate in a different university system (though it can be argued that this is the whole point of study abroad) can take time. Fortunately, you are likely to be assigned an adviser of studies in the UK who may be able to assist you in fine-tuning your programme or your course selection after your arrival. And sometimes having a different background is an advantage rather than a problem. Tutors generally feel that students with different sets of knowledge and different perspectives bring something extra to the class.

THE VALUE OF STUDY ABROAD

Study abroad shares to some degree the benefits of all international study in enabling you to become more sensitive to another culture, more at ease with cultural practice, more sophisticated in your cultural understanding and more relaxed in international company. In a global world, that has benefits for you, not least in employment. The value of study abroad in encouraging internationalism also appeals to governments. This is obvious from the fact that the European Union now funds various inter-Community programmes, like Erasmus and Socrates, on the grounds that they foster a sense of European identity and facilitate vocational mobility amongst graduates within the European Union. Other international bodies have also sought to emulate these internationalist goals, the Commonwealth, the Asian-Pacific states and the North American union amongst them, though so far without the same degree of supportive funding and without generating the same amount of interest.

For some students the greatest appeal of study abroad programmes is that they allow you to experience the benefits of international study without the time commitment (and sometimes without the costs) of full-degree study. But this is also the main drawback. Study abroad is distinctly time-limited. Often students find that they have just begun to feel at home in their new environment and to be getting the most out of their studies when it is time to return. Generally, too, study abroad programmes do not involve any award from the host institution other than a transcript which sets out the courses taken and the grades obtained. This can make the studies seem less formal and less significant. But a number of students on study abroad programmes do return later to undertake post-graduate studies. This suggests that even a short experience can have a lasting impact.

Non-credit courses

Some students choose to study abroad without counting the study towards their home degrees. They simply seek a leave of absence from their home institution and then apply directly to study in the UK on a visiting student or part-course basis. Their situation is identical in most respects to credit-seeking students, except that they have to undertake all the work of applying on their own. They may also be freer in making their course selection since they are not bound by the rules which govern credit transfer. They do, of course, in taking leave, thereby extend the time taken to obtain their degree at home and they must find the costs to undertake this. Some graduate students also apply to study abroad undergraduate pro-grammes, largely so as to be able to study courses which were not available to them in their home degrees or, once they are in employment, as an aspect of their continuing profes-sional development. Most UK institutions have limits on the numbers of such places they can make available but are otherwise prepared to entertain applications.

Non-traditional courses

The choice of what is available in the UK for international students is not limited to what is on offer for local students. There are 'enclave' or 'island' programmes, open only to international students, and usually not open to locals. These often employ some UK teachers and are sometimes held in university premises but are designed to be part of overseas study programmes, not of local ones. Many such courses provide, for example, an introduction to British or European civilisation for those unfamiliar with this area of studies. Visits to local sites and institutions are frequently included in the programme. Often these programmes are concentrated in the summer when the students (and supervisory staff from the home institution) can be mobile without interrupting their regular studies. There are also special programmes for students which include some kind of work placement or exposure to local employment. The intention is to add to the studies knowledge you gain from working in some specific vocational context in the UK, such as in business or in political life. You are more likely to hear about UK-based island programmes and placement courses from your home institution, but can always ask directly, too.

SOME QUESTIONS

What value would study abroad have for you? Has it any evident advantages or disadvantages for you over full-degree study? If study abroad is recognised in your institution, where do you find out about it?

7 FINANCE AND FUNDING

FEE COSTS

A major consideration for every international student, even for those in possession of scholarships, is the question of cost. To compare costs internationally is never easy. Two areas need particular attention: fee costs and living costs. Fee costs are the costs charged for the tuition. In the UK international student fees are likely to vary by institution (the more prestigious tending on the whole to charge more) and also by region (London is obviously the most expensive place in the UK and fee costs usually reflect this). They also vary by discipline. Here there are three basic categories: non-laboratory-based academic subjects; laboratory-based subjects; and clinical (medical-related) subjects. If a course emphasises the scientific basis of medicine, it may well be classified as 'laboratory based' in fee terms; if it emphasises the social-scientific, it may appear as 'non-laboratory based'. As these examples show, the classification of courses is not always straightforward and may need to be checked. You should also bear in mind that fee costs rise annually, usually in line with inflation. Inflation has been low for some time in the UK though that is not guaranteed for evermore. You need also to be certain that all other costs relating immediately to your studies, such as equipment or field trips, have been included. This cannot be assumed, particularly for postgraduates, where what are called 'course costs' can often be quite substantial.

It seems to be agreed that UK international fees cost less than those of private institutions in many other developed countries but are above those of some public or state-provided institutions. This partly depends, however, on whether or not the student is studying in her or his own country since many public institutions charge higher fees to those from outside their country or state. UK costs are, of course, significantly above those in less developed countries. It also needs to be kept in mind that course lengths do vary and you must work out the total fee cost for your entire programme. This has to include any necessary preliminary programmes of study, such as access or foundation courses, which also have a cost. Postgraduate research courses generally charge fees only for the minimum period, which can be one year or two years or three years. If, as sometimes happens, you take longer than the specified minimum period to complete the programme, you are likely still to be charged the minimum amount in fees but will, of course, face increased living costs.

Fee status

There are two categories of fee-payers in the UK, domestic and international. Domestic student fees are usually considerably less than those charged to international students, reflecting the fact that UK students (and their parents) make a further contribution to state educational costs through the taxation system. For the purpose of charging fees, the distinction between a domestic and an international student is defined by law. As with all laws, this produces problems of interpretation, 'grey areas', which result in disputes. Many students suppose that a 'domestic' student simply means a student holding a British passport. This is not, in fact, the case. To be eligible for domestic status, everyone (including local passport holders) needs to be able to establish a 'relevant connection' with the UK. This generally means showing that you have been resident in the UK for three years immediately before beginning your studies and are settled there and have not been resident simply for the purpose of receiving full-time education. Students who are citizens of European Union countries are also defined as 'domestic' for fee purposes providing they have been resident within the European Economic Area for three years immediately before beginning their studies. They too, of course, must have been resident for some purpose other than receiving full-time education.

These rules do, however, involve a number of technical terms which are subject to legal interpretation. There are also a number of exceptions which are allowed (for example, European Union citizens unable to fulfil the residency requirement because of temporary employment outside the EEA are excepted) and refugees are accorded an exceptional status. All of this can make the distinction between domestic and international uncertain. Fortunately, it is sufficiently clear for most people to be sure which would apply to them. But, if you are in any doubt, you may need to have the matter investigated. Most universities will agree to consider your case and will give you a ruling on which category they feel applies to you. Their ruling, of course, will determine what you will be charged, since the fees are paid directly to the university on registration.

LIVING COSTS

Living costs are more difficult to calculate than fees since they depend in part on lifestyle. If your intention is to live at a highly fashionable address, eat out in the best restaurants each evening and entertain in regal style, your costs will not be the same as for someone with more modest tastes. In university-provided accommodation (which is usually subsidised in the UK), the cost may well be less than for those living in the private sector (which is not), though there are no hard-and-fast rules here. If the institution is in the north of England, the expenses will almost certainly be less than if it is in the southeast. Any figures that are quoted, however, need to be treated with caution. They mean nothing until you know how they have been calculated. You must examine them closely. Some may represent the minimum required for sheer survival; others may anticipate some occasional extravagances. It may also be necessary to build in some unfamiliar costs, such as cold weather clothing, if that is not something that you already regard as a seasonal necessity. On the other hand, medical treatment under the National Health Service is normally free, which avoids heavy health insurance costs.

The safest conclusion is that the UK has living costs comparable with those in much of the developed world. Where there are likely to be advantages is in the concessions which are allowed specifically for students. One already mentioned is subsidised university-provided accommodation. In the UK, there are also often student concessions for the cinema and theatre, restaurants and shops, sports facilities and tourist sites. Public museums and galleries in the UK are also free for the most part. Most universities and colleges provide their own student entertainment programmes, films, theatre and sports, at substantially discounted prices. Almost all will have student refectories, which provide food at rates students find easier to afford. These extras, and the fact that the academic programmes are reasonably intensive and concentrated, are what give the UK its claim to being financially competitive.

EMPLOYMENT

Another financial benefit is that you are allowed to take a job and to earn while in the UK, providing you are studying for over six months. There are some exceptions, generally relating to students from countries experiencing difficult diplomatic relations with Britain. But such exceptions are few. If you are studying for six months or less, however, you are not automatically conferred with the right to work and will need to ask the immigration officer for permission on arrival. Your spouse also has the right to work (unless you have been refused). You will find further information on the Internet about this, at www.dfes.gov.uk/international-students/wituk.shtml. You can usually work up to twenty hours a week in term-time and longer during vacations. But, against this, students are only eligible for temporary jobs and these tend not to be the best paid. Nor is it guaranteed that everyone will find a job. And intensive studies mean that in any case there is only limited time for working. The right to work is best seen as a reserve, something that you may be able to fall back upon, rather than something which should automatically be included in your initial calculations.

EXCHANGE RATES

There is another financial point to be considered – exchange rates. These make all calculations very difficult. The rate at which you calculate your costs before you go to the UK may not be the rate that prevails throughout your period of study. Currencies fluctuate, sometimes quite wildly, in relation to each other. All calculations should therefore allow for some element of chance variation in both directions – up and down. When a UK university admits you, it is obliged to check in advance that you have shown that you have all the necessary funding to cover not only your fees but your living costs (though no one is required to bring all this funding with them to the UK immediately). It may ask for proof of that funding, for example in bank statements, a letter from your sponsor or evidence that you hold a scholarship. Sometimes pre-payment of a portion of fees is recommended. These precautions are taken fundamentally because of the requirements of the UK immigration authorities. The government is concerned to ensure that if you are admitted as a student, you do not become, in the official phrase, 'a burden on the state'. That means checking that you have sufficient funds to cover all your costs. Being required to have proof of your funding at least ensures that you have to know in advance how much you will need. In times of hardship, the institution may be able to offer some relief, by rescheduling payments, by allowing payment by instalments, even by finding funds to assist. But it is wise not to rely on any of this. Instead some allowance for an unforeseen difficulty should be made, so that, should any crisis arise, you can surmount it with confidence.

FUNDING THE STUDY

For most students who don't have ample private means, the search for funding is a major concern. Only a fraction of all the students qualified to study abroad are in fact able to find the resources which permit them to do so. Though the UK does offer some scholarships, not everyone can expect to obtain one. It is necessary therefore to spend time both deciding how much the studies will cost and how the necessary funds are going to be found. If you have private funding, from parents or from relatives or friends, there is still a need to know how much will be required and surely there is also a need for everyone to ensure that you use your funds wisely. If there is no private funding or not enough, it becomes necessary to look for support elsewhere. Unfortunately, the likelihood of success is very far from certain. You may feel deserving of support, but you will probably need stamina and luck, as well as a good academic record and a good personal profile, to have any real hope of success.

Local funds

In most countries in the world, there are some scholarships or loans on very favourable terms which are open only to local or 'home' students and which are intended for study in other countries. It is necessary to find out what those are, what the criteria are for eligibility and how to apply for them. Most students start their search by talking first to advisers at their university, college or school. Lecturers and teachers will have a good idea of the range of provision available and will be able to judge how likely you are to qualify for support. The scholarships may be from governmental sources. If so, these are generally easy to trace by contacting your local education department. Some international awards, like Commonwealth Scholarships, are also made through individual national governments, so information on those, too, should be available from that source.

There may also be private sources, and they are much less easy to trace. Teachers again may be able to help or friends who have already studied abroad. They may know of some sources from personal experience or from other students who have found funding locally. Some British Council offices keep a file on the local sources of support which students have used in the past to obtain funding to study in the UK. Sometimes there are books on funding in local libraries and a kind librarian should be able to point the way. This search for funding at home requires energy and effort, with no guarantee of success. But it should not be neglected, since many donors prefer to offer their awards locally rather than in the country in which the award will be held.

In some cases, loans on favourable terms will be offered instead of or in addition to scholarships. As in the UK (where such loans are available only to British undergraduate students), these, though often provided by banks, are likely to have been negotiated through the local government. Arrangements for the loans will always include terms about how they must be repaid and there may also be further conditions relating to your future employment. Sometimes the agency making the loan will require the agreement of the receiving university in the UK, which will be asked to submit periodic reports on your attendance and progress. In addition, some students (or their families) are able to obtain commercial loans in order to study in the UK. Needless to say, as with all other borrowing, this involves a considerable risk. Anyone embarking on it would want first to have professional financial advice.

UK scholarships

The bulk of international students rely on scholarships obtained locally or on private funding sources. But some are able to find support in the UK. Nearly all UK scholarship awards are competitive. Most of them are aimed at students of ability, often outstanding ability. Some do take other factors into account, such as your financial means or the particular difficulty you face in finding funding. Few UK institutions would claim, however, that their policy on international admissions is entirely means-blind, that is that they can judge each applicant exclusively on ability and then provide funding for all those who reach the required standard. But there are funds provided by the UK government, by businesses and companies and by the institutions themselves with the intention of getting closer to that ideal. One of the largest of these funds is the Chevening programme, which blends private and public sources to create scholarships, chiefly for one-year taught master's degree students. There are also awards made available by businesses and companies, by charitable bodies and by the individual institutions, all in their own names. These cover studies at all levels, though in general there are few sources of support for undergraduates. Some are full, some part scholarships; some provide a contribution only to fees, some to both fees and living costs. Some are aimed at new students, others at students already on a course. Your local British Council office (and its web-site) is often the best place to look for general information on UK scholarship provision. That will point you in the right direction.

There are also a number of books and pamphlets that contain relevant information on funding sources for study in the UK and some also include worldwide sources of funding, open to students studying in any country. UKCOSA (the United Kingdom Council for Overseas Student Affairs) offers some helpful comments about all this on its web-site (www.ukcosa.org.uk). It is also a good idea, once you have decided to apply, to approach your individual institution. Some information about funding is quite likely to be printed in the prospectus. Your university, like the British Council, will also know what has proved successful in the past. This knowledge is often used to compile lists of possible funding sources in the UK and abroad and sometimes you can find this on the institution's web-site. The university will also know of funds specific to the institution itself, if any such exist.

UK government awards

There are two principal governmental awards in the UK for international students, both aimed at postgraduate students, Chevening awards, information about which is always distributed through British Council offices, and the British Government's Overseas Research Student (ORS) awards. In fee terms, ORS awards are less generous than Chevenings. They generally provide the difference between the fees levied on 'domestic' and 'international' students, so in effect reducing your fee costs to those of a local student. They are also prestigious and sometimes an ORS award will encourage another funding body to offer its support. As already mentioned, Chevening awards are aimed mainly at one-year taught master's. If you apply for a Chevening award, you will be expected to have a very strong academic record. You must also already have received an offer of a place in a UK institution. And one of the principal elements in these awards is that you must have shown yourself to be a worthy citizen of your country by making some distinct contribution to local society. Those who win these awards are seen as likely future leaders of their country in some walk of life. Chevenings, therefore, have more than an educational significance. This is reflected in the fact that they are mainly funded by the British Foreign Office (the name is taken from the Foreign Secretary's official country residence) and by the universities. By contrast, ORS awards, which are largely government funded, are awarded more purely on the basis of academic excellence. They are offered through UK universities who must nominate candidates they think worthy of the award. The first approach for anyone in search of an ORS award therefore has to be to the university where you are hoping to study.

University awards

Many universities in the UK have scholarships of their own which they award annually. Although almost all of these are hugely competitive, some are used to support students already on course who have shown promise and whom the institutions would like to encourage to continue further with their studies. Others are offered to those who are progressing well but who have encountered unexpected financial difficulties. In recent times, a small number have also been offered in support of recruiting efforts. A university which wishes to attract students from a particular country or into a particular course or discipline may, for example, offer a scholarship exclusively to students on that basis. Such scholarships are sometimes 'partial' rather than 'full', meaning that they cover only some part of the fee cost or living cost or will be awarded for only part of the study period. They are sometimes described as bursaries rather than scholarships to indicate that they are seen as a form of assistance rather than of full support. In practice, universities find that they receive far more applications for their scholarships than they can hope to satisfy. As a result, they often make it a rule that you must have applied for and been provisionally granted a place on the course before you can be considered for a scholarship. Many also expect you to apply simultaneously for other scholarships, such as the government's ORS awards, in an effort to make their own funds go further.

Applying for a scholarship

Almost all scholarships require applications long in advance of the period when the study begins (or sometimes long after – if they are open only to students already on course in their first or later years of study). When they are available to beginners you should normally expect to have to apply at least nine months or a year ahead of the start of your studies. This, like the situation for visas and university places, clearly indicates the importance of planning ahead. In all cases, applications require thought. To be successful, they must be presented in the most persuasive way. Those making the decisions on scholarship applications will not necessarily have an intimate knowledge of the educational system in every country. If ability is the principal criterion, your application should set out the grounds which best illustrate your claim to be an outstanding student. It is particularly helpful if reference can be made to evidence which is clearly objective and not simply a matter of personal opinion. Again it helps a lot if you can give your ranking within a class or any awards you have received whose status is widely recognised or which can be explained. And it is a good idea to brief your referees on what the institution is looking for from them, if there is any way of knowing this.

While funds from official sources are generally awarded on the bases of ability and need, private funds may have a variety of other considerations, too, relating to the wishes of the donor. An effort needs to be made to discover what these are in order to ensure that the application makes reference to the most appropriate evidence, namely the aspects of your career which match the donor's expectations or stipulations. If you are applying for university funds, it is only common sense to try and show some knowledge of the institution itself and of the course for which you are seeking support. Donors may be suspicious if you give the impression of merely being in search of funding from wherever it is to be found. As with applications generally, a knowledge of what you are applying for and who you are applying to is a distinct asset in being able to present a convincing case.

SOME QUESTIONS

How much is it going to cost you to complete your studies in the UK? How are you going to find the funds to cover this amount? What are the fixed elements in your budget and what things are uncertain? What safeguards do you need to include?

8 PREPARING TO MOVE

ACCEPTANCES: UNDERGRADUATES

Once your application has been submitted, there is usually a delay before the result is known. If you have applied for entry as an undergraduate, the delay may be partly explained by UCAS procedures. The application has to be forwarded to a central location and then distributed to the individual institutions so that each receives it at the same time and has the same opportunity to consider it. It also takes time for the institutions to which you have applied to ensure that they can select the best candidates and can match their acceptances to the number of places available. But most applicants soon receive a response from each of their chosen institutions, usually within a few weeks. This can make you an outright offer, a conditional offer or a rejection. Of course there may be greater delays for the most popular institutions and in the most popular subjects. But institutions are aware that their attractiveness relates partly to their ability to respond as rapidly as their competitors, and delays are generally kept to a minimum. If you receive an offer which needs to be confirmed when later results from examinations become available, you will then have a further wait, but matters generally proceed routinely thereafter. The system also allows you, if you do not do as well as you expected in your exams, to appeal; but as a rule it soon becomes clear when the offer is final and all conditions have been met.

ACCEPTANCES: POSTGRADUATES

For postgraduates, the delay between submission and offer is sometimes lengthier, particularly where the university insists on a direct correspondence with referees or asks for supplementary information. Since individual supervisors will also be involved in the selection, and some of them will be otherwise engaged on their own research and teaching when the applications arrive, it can take time to get a final decision on every application. Yet, once again, within a few weeks of receipt of all required information, a response should be forthcoming. If you have still not heard after a reasonable period of time, say within a month, you should write and enquire. But do make allowance for delays occasioned by the post or by public holidays and do remember that an application is not complete until all the references have been submitted and all required documents have been included.

JOINING INSTRUCTIONS

Once an offer of a place is received which you wish to take up, preparations can begin for the time to be spent in the UK. The first important consideration is to write back to the university or college and accept the offer, after which a final letter of admission will be sent. The letter of admission is the formal document that is normally required for immigration entry. Being a student entitles you to a special visa status in the UK, different from that for tourists or for those seeking employment, and it is this status which you need the final letter in order to obtain. Along with the final letter or shortly afterwards, other instructions, sometimes called joining instructions, are also likely to be sent. These documents are concerned with simple practicalities – how to reach the institution, how to apply for accommodation, when to register for the start of the academic programme, and so on. Joining instructions normally arrive in good time to allow you to make your preparations. But that may not be immediately. If there is any particular urgency about receiving any of these documents, you ought to make that known when accepting the offer.

ENTRY VISAS

Once you have received your final letter of acceptance, you must ensure that you have made the necessary preparations to enter the UK as a student. Your local British embassy, high commission or consulate will have the latest information about this. For many students, depending on nationality, preparation is simplicity itself and requires no formal letter of authority. Citizens of the European Economic Area, for example, are entitled to study in the UK and can prove this simply by showing their passport to an immigration official on arrival. If you have already obtained your passport or national identity card, you are set. Students from many other countries in the world, including the USA, are also permitted to study in the UK without any visa, though they do need a special stamp which will be put in their passport on arrival. If you are in this category and would like your entry guaranteed, you can obtain an entry certificate from the local British embassy or consulate to confirm your student status before you travel to the UK. The advantage of obtaining the certificate is that, should any unforeseen difficulty crop up on arrival, it can then be used to gain entry and so to allow time to sort out the problem. To obtain it, there is a form which has to be completed and a charge is made for the service. You will also need a passport, a final letter of acceptance and some proof of your ability to fund the studies in the UK. The entry certificate which is then issued is, however, only an extra safeguard. Providing everything is normal, the likelihood of any difficulty arising is so remote that many students seem unwilling to bother with it, probably because of the time and paperwork involved.

There are a number of countries, like China, for example, where a visa is required formally, and this has to be obtained in advance. The countries on the 'visa required' list do change, but the British embassy or high commission will be able to say which are on it, if there is any doubt. The current list is also available on the Internet (www.ukvisas.gov.uk). If a visa is required, it can take quite a long time to obtain. When the studies are going to take more than six months, the visa request will in many cases have to be referred back to the UK. This may mean a matter of months rather than weeks before the embassy receives permission to issue the visa, even when the application is approved. The visa authorities will also want to be certain that the applicant is genuinely going to be a student and is not someone simply seeking permission to enter the UK for some other purpose. The visa officers in the embassy or high commission are therefore entitled to send for and question the applicant in order to confirm for themselves that she or he has the necessary qualifications to undertake the studies. If this happens, they will want to know what your purpose is in undertaking the studies. They will certainly expect you to be able to answer questions about the course you propose to take, its title, its length, its features. Applying for a visa and attending a visa interview should not cause anyone any concern, but it may require some thought and preparation.

It will also involve supplying the visa authorities with some documents. These will again include the letter of admission issued by the university (usually an offer letter is not enough – they require the final letter, sent out after the acceptance of the offer has been returned). They will obviously need a current passport, which of course you may also have to be obtain if you don't have one already. They will expect proof of your funding, your scholarship grant letter, for example, or a written statement from your sponsor (who might be a relative). The visa officers will want you to have made some calculation of all the costs involved, living as well as fee costs, and to have provided evidence that your funding covers both. They are also allowed to check that you have the necessary skills to cope with studies in the UK and this can include proof of your English language competence. And they may well want to be able to understand the significance of the course selected for your present or future career. It is only sensible to gather this information in advance and to be prepared to present it, if required.

It is already clear that such matters cannot be left until the last minute. It takes time to obtain a passport, time to obtain and complete visa application forms, time to assemble evidence; and, even when all that is done, it takes time before the outcome of the application is known. Most people suggest that you need to begin the work at least six months before you are due to start your course. Working backwards, that means it may be necessary to apply for the course even before the normally recommended six months' deadline. Of course, you can be lucky. Sometimes everything happens very quickly. But that cannot be guaranteed. Being prepared and thinking things out well in advance is much the best approach.

ACCOMMODATION

Once you've got a place to study and your funding is secure, all other problems are likely to be little ones. In the joining instructions, students are often told how best to prepare for their arrival. The most essential requirement is probably that of fixing up accommodation since everyone wants to feel settled as soon as possible. Ideally, finding a place would be better done after arrival when it would be possible to inspect properties and compare prices. Certainly, for those coming only a short distance, a preliminary visit to scout out the land is not a bad idea. For most students, however, it is necessary to compromise and to rely on the information sent by post or provided on the Internet. Most universities can provide accommodation though they are more likely to have more rooms for single students than for couples or families. The information which the institution gives about the location, nature and ambience of its accommodation is usually enough to enable you to make a choice. The advantages of choosing university-provided accommodation are obvious. The accommodation is usually subsidised and is therefore good value. Rooms in dormitories or 'halls of residence' (the more usual British term) and other university-owned or university-run properties offer generally a ready-made community of fellow students, which helps everyone to feel at home and to settle down quickly. Even if the accommodation is in 'flats' (apartments) and is not separated out from local housing, there will still be other students sharing the property to whom you, as a newcomer, can turn for understanding advice and support.

Where university accommodation is not allocated in advance, it will probably be necessary to arrange temporary accommodation before beginning to search in the private accommodation sector (that is, property not owned or managed by the university but supplied on a commercial basis). The usual advice is that those looking for accommodation not just for themselves but also for their partner and children should probably travel alone to the UK, find the accommodation, and then send for the others. Most temporary accommodation is more expensive than long-let accommodation, so it is wise to try and make the search a rapid one. Again the university should be able to provide in advance a good deal of helpful advice on things to do on arrival, newspapers to read, housing agencies to contact and noticeboards to check where available accommodation is advertised. If some preparation can be done before departure, it is more likely that a place will be found quickly. Every university will have an accommodation office and that is where enquiries should begin.

The accommodation on offer in the large private housing market in the UK will be much less standardised than university properties. In consequence, it could be cheaper though it is likely to be more expensive. If it proves necessary to search within the private sector, again most universities will give you a good deal of advice. You might also look to see whether the university web-site has a page for those looking for flatmates. If there is, you can get in touch with those advertising a vacancy and discuss details. In general, it would be unwise to agree to any private lease without first inspecting the property, unless friends or agents can undertake the inspection by proxy. There is clearly a need to be aware of the legal aspects of signing an accommodation contract and your local students' association is the best place to obtain help with this.

It also needs to be borne in mind – as also when accepting accommodation from the university – that renting property involves legal obligations. If the course lasts only for nine months, it may be unwise to take on a contract for twelve. If only a nine months' contract is available and the course lasts for twelve, some thought needs to be given to how matters will be arranged at the end of that first period of tenure. Universities will have a lot of experience of the accommodation needs of students and will usually be sensitive to different requirements. But they too will have to balance their books and so will expect everyone to abide by all the terms in the contract. The private sector landlord may be less experienced in dealing with students and less accommodating, so it is well to be very sure of any commitments involved. 'Read the fine print in the agreement' is sensible advice whenever signing a contract with anyone about anything.

ARRANGING A BANK TRANSFER

It will be very important for you to have access to funds immediately or soon after your arrival. In many countries in the world it is easy to obtain British pounds ('sterling') and it makes sense to have enough for train, bus or taxi fares on arrival and for other immediate expenses concerned with the first few days in the UK. In Britain, quite a lot of use is made of credit cards and all the usual international ones are recognised. There are cash points at banks in every town and city and it may also be possible to obtain small amounts of cash from them using your credit card. You will first have to enquire at home with your own bank in order to obtain any necessary code numbers. Credit cards can also be used in many shops and offices but they are not acceptable for every financial transaction in the UK. It is therefore important that funds are transferred early so that you can get access to cash soon after your arrival. To do this, arrangements have to be made in advance. Any bank should be able to explain how money can be carried abroad or transferred. Sometimes the bank will have branches in the UK or will be able to use a UK bank as its partner. If the funds for the study have been deposited with a local bank in your home country, the manager may also be able to supply you with a letter which can be used in opening an account. You can also use it to show to the immigration authorities in the UK. This letter should attest to your financial position and indicate that you have all the means required for the whole study period.

At least one expense can be paid even before departure. Most universities hold their fee account in a UK bank and can provide details of that account so that funds to cover the first fee payment can be transferred and paid in advance. Again a bank manager will advise on how soon this needs to be done to ensure that the transfer has been effected before you are due to register for studies. It is important to keep any documents about the transaction to show the university authorities and as proof that the payment has been made. Fee payment in advance is not, however, a requirement (except where institutions ask for a deposit). If you prefer to pay everything in the UK, you need only ensure that your funds have been transferred and that you have access to them on arrival.

OTHER NEEDS

Many students ask for advice about what to bring with them or to send ahead. A little thought needs to be given to lifestyle in the UK in order to decide what items would be useful to take. If the university doesn't provide a guide on this, there are many tourist handbooks for the UK, usually available in local libraries, which will serve instead. All of them include information which will be helpful, however different your circumstances are from those of a tourist. The rain falls equally on both and the electricity power points are also a shared experience. By reading guidebooks, you can also learn what attracts others to the city or area in which your studies will be conducted and that can be interesting in itself. But the main purpose is to discover what tourists are advised to wear, to eat, to read and to do while staying in the UK.

It makes sense to pay particular attention to clothing needs and to the different clothing requirements for different times of the year. Airlines have limits on the amount of luggage which passengers can take with them on the plane and it can be expensive to send things unaccompanied. It is often the case, of course, that the things needed in the UK will be cheaper if bought locally where local requirement has produced a local demand. Some things are also better obtained locally because they are designed with local circumstances in mind. But it is possible to avoid a bit of expense by correctly guessing which amongst your current possessions will serve you equally well in the UK. Since Britain has four seasons, most kinds of clothes will be useful at some time in the year even if they were bought for life in the tropics. Other things you might use, like a small supply of paper and pens, can also be helpful in the first weeks until it proves possible to find the best value local suppliers. Students often feel attached to their hobbies, and sports equipment and musical instruments also sometimes make the journey from home – though it is possible to buy a snorkelling outfit in the UK and a cello probably won't come within your airline luggage allowance. There is no point in taking too much. The world is so small nowadays that even 'local' proprietary brands are often available everywhere.

Most student enquiries about luggage seem to relate to computers, an area which develops so quickly that the advice given one minute seems already out of date the next. Clearly laptop computers, which are designed to be light and portable, are not a problem to take, though it is necessary to check up with the university on their usage in the UK, if there is any doubt about it. Anything heavier or more cumbersome is probably best left at home. Most institutions can give students access to a computer during the day.

Special needs provision

Those with medical needs and those with a disability may want to correspond with their institution before leaving to make sure that those things which need to be brought are packed and those things which can be conveniently supplied locally are not. In making an application to a university, anyone with a disability should already have alerted the institution to his or her requirements. This applies as much to classroom or study provision as to accommodation needs. Many UK institutions pride themselves on what they can do for students with disabilities. But they need to know the nature of the disability in order to ensure that everything is in place. A lecture scheduled in a room which cannot be accessed by those in wheelchairs, for example, can be moved elsewhere if the institution knows that this is going to be needed. It is much harder to move it if nothing is known until the student turns up at the first lecture. If you correspond with your institution before your departure, you can ensure that its officials are clear about what they need to provide. You should ask what is available, what has been done for others in the past and what challenges may still have to be met.

BOOKING A FLIGHT

Most of us have no difficulty in booking a flight since we take the advice of a travel agent on what is most convenient, what is the best value and what most customers prefer. Nowadays, many people use the Internet to make bookings and can achieve savings by doing so. The important consideration is to compare prices, routes and timings. If the travel to the UK involves a considerable distance, a flight which has several stops or which requires a transfer from one plane to another *en route* can be quite tiring, unless a stop-over is part of the arrangement. But the inconvenience may be compensated for by lower cost. Delays in transfer are another consideration. If there is a delay for half a day before a connecting flight is available, you will be exhausted by the time you arrive.

There are many international airports in the UK. You also have the option of choosing an airline that uses an arrival airport outside the UK (in Amsterdam, Brussels, Paris or Frankfurt, for example). Often this same airline, by itself or through a partnership agreement with other airlines, can then provide a convenient connecting flight onward direct to your destination airport in the UK, usually at a discounted price. Many airlines using one of the London airports as a hub can also offer this onward discounted travel (if London is not your final destination). You need to work out the total cost, rather than look just at the long-haul element of your journey. Those travelling from within Europe also have the option of taking a train or boat as well as flying, which greatly extends the range of possibilities and prices.

If it is possible to avoid arriving very late in the evening, this should certainly be done, unless the institution has been alerted and has said that it can make the necessary arrangements to cope. In most countries in the world, things shut down at some point in the evening. All students should tell their institution when and where they will arrive and, unless the information is in the joining instructions, you should ask whether any 'meet and greet' service is provided. These are usually student-run reception committees which arrange to be at the airport or station to welcome you. They will give you instructions about how to get to your residence or institution. They may also be able to tell you (unless you've received the information already) how to obtain entry to your residence and how to make arrangements to settle in. Nothing is happier when travelling abroad than to be greeted on first arrival by welcoming, smiling faces, all hoping to be of help. Nothing is less happy than to arrive exhausted and confused at a deserted airport at dead of night to find that there is no transport into town till morning. It is a circumstance that can usually be avoided with a bit of advance planning.

SOME QUESTIONS

What documents will you need to prepare for immigration purposes in the UK? How long will it take you to obtain what you need? How much of this can you get ready before you get an acceptance and how much will have to wait? Who would be your best source of advice on travel arrangements?

9 ARRIVAL AND FIRST DAYS

ARRIVAL

New international students are faced on arrival by so many novel situations that the first few days usually pass in a blur. To try and anticipate what each student will experience at this stage is not entirely easy since individual institutions will have their own peculiarities. But some things seem fairly general and are perhaps worth knowing about before departure. For example, there are formalities to be completed on arrival, the journey to a new home to be undertaken and settling in to be begun. For those who are also suffering from jet lag while trying to get to know something of the peculiarities of the place in which they have come to live, the experience can be quite disorientating. For others, it is just as often entirely exhilarating. Students in the UK are naturally gregarious though also socially cautious, and new arrivals sometimes find that they are swept up in an endless round of get-togethers or are left puzzled by why their neighbours have not yet come to call.

Immigration

Everyone arriving in a foreign country first has to proceed through immigration. This should all be a perfectly simple and straightforward process, and usually it is. But when those arriving are coming not as tourists but as temporary residents, as all students are, the checks made can take longer and be more onerous. On arrival, you are likely to be tired after a long flight and probably excited, so the need to follow what the immigration officer is saying can be quite trying. But providing you are alert enough to deal with any questions and that you have looked out and kept with you the necessary documentation (particularly your passport, letter of admission and evidence of funding), all should be well.

Citizens of the European Union usually have the briefest time at immigration. Frequently, the immigration official will simply wave you through with only the most cursory look at your passport. Those from countries which are not required to obtain a visa in advance will be detained only a little longer. You will have your passport stamped with a written indication that you have been granted the right to reside in the UK as a student for a certain period. Quite often these days, the period will cover the entire length of the course and you will need to tell the immigration official how long that will be. But the permission can be for much shorter periods, too, if, for any reason, the official judges that to be desirable. There is no problem with this beyond the fact that it means you then have to apply for an extension to your 'visa' once the first period comes towards an end, and that involves a certain amount of paperwork and effort. Those who come from countries on the 'visa required' list will also have their passport stamped, with a written indication of the period for which the residence permission has been granted. Again, this is renewable if the period granted is less than is required to complete the course, but again you will have to gather evidence and complete the necessary forms. There may also be a statement on the stamp to say that you are not allowed to take employment, a matter which can relate to your country of origin or to your particular individual circumstances. Immigration officials, like tax inspectors, are unloved. But they are not trying to impede anyone's entry (unless there are plans to do so illegally). They are trying to get things right, according to the law and the evidence that you put before them. If you are clear and direct with them, all should be well.

Getting there

In all probability, you will have been sent instructions by your institution about how to get from the point of entry to your new place of residence. This needs to be observed. Airports, railway terminals and docks are amongst the least engaging places in the world. They are often well supplied with help desks, but, once you find one, the person at the front of the queue seems to have embarked on an account of their life story to the person behind the counter. For those arriving at or near the start of the academic year, there is a good chance that there may be a waiting student reception committee. Their help should certainly be sought, even if it is clearly meant for another institution or another category of student. There's a natural comradeship, a fraternity, within the academic community, which is most useful on such occasions. Uni-formed staff are also usually very helpful, though not if they are there to guard the building. If anyone offers advice which is hard to understand, the solution is to ask again and to go on asking until everything is clear. Usually there is a relatively cheap and convenient way on to the next or final destination. For those in any doubt about what this might be, it is best to ask someone: 'What is the best way to get to . . . ?' Unless you've approached a taxi driver (who may have a vested interest), the answer is likely to be highly reliable.

SETTLING INTO ACCOMMODATION

Those who have arranged a place in university-provided accommodation will presumably take occupation of that immediately on arrival and then begin to find their way around. This assumes, of course, that you have followed the university's directions on the date of your arrival or have negotiated another date acceptable to the university autho-rities. Some students may be in temporary accommodation, having agreed with the university on the date by which they will move to their permanent place. Or you may have taken temporary accommodation while beginning to search for somewhere more permanent. Those in the last situation need immediately to get in touch with the university's accommodation service to see what help they can provide and must keep up this contact until they are permanently settled. You will also need to begin your search of university noticeboards, local newspaper 'To Let' columns or housing agency lists to see what is available within your price range and desired location. Since large numbers of other students are likely to be doing the same at precisely the same time, this requires stamina. When you find something that seems attractive and at a suitable price, it may be sensible to agree to the deal verbally, but the earlier warnings about not signing anything until the fine print has been read still apply.

SECURITY AND MONEY

On first arrival students need to be conscious of their security. Britain is generally a safe country but you must still be sensible and careful. Wallet, keys and university cards need to be looked after. There is often a casual bohemia about student life but it is wise not to drop into this too soon. Doors need to be secured initially, belongings safeguarded, valuables protected. At some early point it is best to make arrangements to open a bank account at a convenient branch of a bank so as to avoid carrying around large quantities of cash. Convenience might mean being close to where you live or close to where you will attend classes. If money has been sent from home in advance, it may now have to be moved to the most convenient branch and it may be necessary to get access to it through opening an account. Opening different accounts for different needs may be possible, so as to be able to write cheques or to pay by credit card, for example. All this requires you to supply evidence of the fact that you are in good financial standing and probably also that you are a recognised 'matriculated' student. As when coming through immigration, it is useful to take some documentation along when you approach a bank. The bank, though it clearly has an interest, will be an expert source of advice on how to handle money in the UK and it will give guidance, if required. The Students' Association will also be able to advise on money matters (and on so many other matters).

THE ORIENTATION PROCESS

An orientation programme for new students held before classes start is nowadays virtually universal in all institutions. Information about this event is likely to be sent out along with the joining instructions. It traditionally takes place in the days immediately preceding the start of term (which, of course, means that those who want to take part in it have to arrange to arrive at that time and not just at the start of term). In some cases, the programme is organised by the Students' Association or Students' Union and often the information about it comes directly from them. Usually it is necessary to apply separately to attend, since orientation events cannot be compulsory unless they take place in term-time, and a small charge may be involved to cover some part of the cost. But it is often possible to register for the event after arrival, providing of course that you have got there in good time. Orientations are generally very useful and enjoyable occasions and everyone is strongly advised to attend.

The orientation programme is designed to provide new arrivals with a basic introduction to life as a student in each particular institution. This is likely to consist of several elements. An official welcome by some senior university figures is standard. There are also likely to be some talks to help everyone understand the institution more fully. Outside the university, a familiarisation event is usually organised to allow newcomers to get to know the town or city in which they have come to live. It is also extremely likely that there will be a great many social occasions to enable you, as a new student, to fraternise with other students so that you can begin to make friends and feel more at home. Some institutions use the orientation also to provide an introduction to some aspects of studying (though this may come later in term-time). Quite frequently there is a special session exclusively for international students and indeed there may be a whole programme, lasting from a day to a week, on that basis. If so, the programme may well also contain an introduction to life in the UK and some tips about how to cope with local cultural peculiarities. At some point international students are likely to be brought together with domestic students in a general orientation for all new arrivals. Postgraduates will probably have shorter orientation programmes (it is assumed that you are already familiar with much that undergraduates find mysterious) and ones more focused on the nature of your studies.

The orientation will also provide occasions when new students will meet with students in their second or later years. While the central point of student life is, of course, to study for a qualification, the fact that everyone becomes a member of an academic community (which is not generally true for those studying by distance learning, for example) is judged equally important. This is why during orientation older students target new students with an invitation to join their societies or to participate in events they have arranged or to give their support to causes which form part of student life in the institution and for which they are acting as recruiting officers. The usual advice is not to try to do too much and not to sign up to too many projects too quickly. There will be opportunities later in the term to join almost all of these organisations, for those still interested if you find that you have the time to devote to them. But this is an excellent opportunity to learn something about what students in the institution are interested in and to get to grips with the bonding process which lies behind the creation of any student community.

ARRANGING COURSES

During the week before studies commence, perhaps while the orientation programme is going on, new students are required to register in the university. You must ensure that you have been allocated a place in the various classes that you intend to take. This may all have been pre-arranged with merely the paperwork remaining to be completed. But for undergraduates, at least in most cases, there will need to be some further discussion. Each student is likely to be allocated an academic adviser. This adviser will want to meet you, to go over your programme with you and to complete the necessary bureaucratic processes on your behalf. Although this is probably the busiest part of the academic year and it is very difficult to find time for extensive discussions, it is important that these meetings with an academic adviser are given a very high priority. They are one of the key means by which the university opens up all its various support services to every student. The adviser is likely to be in touch with all the academics and all the social welfare officers who can be of help to you, right across the institution. Since things are so pressured at this time, you need especially to establish when, where and how you will be able to contact your adviser again should you require her or his advice in the future.

As part of the process of registration, undergraduates and taught postgraduates need to give some thought to any optional courses that they can undertake, since the discussion is likely to include that. They must also be prepared for a question about their longer-term plans, no matter how vague and insubstantial these may be. The adviser's task is in part to suggest ways in which your interests and enthusiasms can be matched to what the institution provides. If you have no certain plans but many vague ones, these are likely to be an equally helpful starting point. Discussing those will help your adviser to understand what would suit you best.

INFORMATION OVERLOAD

Coming to an agreement with an adviser about your initial period of studies (which can cover a term or a semester or a year) does not end the process of becoming a student. Much time is likely to be spent in queues, finalising registration, getting membership cards for the library and for the computer services and attending official events. At the same time, from all quarters within the institution and from many outside it, comes a bombardment of more information for new arrivals. Some of this can be safely ignored. If, for example, it comes from commercial booksellers trying to persuade you to buy books, it is wise not to respond until classes actually commence. At that point, detailed reading lists are likely to be provided with full information on what is thought essential; and it may be that last year's compulsory text (which you had thought of buying) has already been replaced by something more recent. Students complain of information overload during orientation and of the difficulty of sorting out the wheat from the chaff. Yet much of what is communicated, if it is important, is likely to be repeated at a later stage in your studies. The problem of information overload is probably best met by treating everything except the official matters quite light-heartedly.

SOCIALISING

As mentioned, you may find that your first weeks in university consist of a frenzy of endless socialising or you may feel that you missed opportunities to meet others by being unsure about what to do. This seems partly to relate to different cultural expectations and customs. Student life in the UK is generally extremely friendly and sociable. But it is accepted that everyone is entitled to a certain amount of privacy and solitude, if that is your preferred choice. Most students find that initially they want to build up a social circle quite quickly. If that is the goal, there is never any problem about taking the initiative and knocking on a neighbour's door yourself and effecting introductions. Beyond this, an early trip to the Students' Union or wherever students traditionally get together can help to push the boat out. In the orientation period, there are usually students there whose job is specifically to help new arrivals to get to know others. One of the benefits of attending the international orientation is that it allows new students to recognise each other. New students are likely to be especially friendly, since they are sharing much the same experiences and have a shared need for company. It is also a good idea for you to try and meet others from your own country. This is often neglected in the desire for integration. But it can be infinitely easier to break into a new society by being able to talk about it to someone from your own. In time, of course, everyone's social circle will expand much further, particularly once teaching starts and you begin to participate in groups and classes.

HEALTH ISSUES

Unless studying medicine or in some way exposed to the risk of infection, you are not expected routinely to provide evidence about your health on arrival in the UK. Nor are you generally required to submit yourself to any medical tests (though students do sometimes volunteer to participate in some medical trials). But you are expected to register with a GP (General Practitioner or family doctor) and in this have a choice about which GP to select. There are long lists in the local phone book. Most students either register with the university health service, where there is one, or with a practice located near their homes or near their place of study. If you are studying for more than six months, medical treatment is free in the UK for all illnesses which arise during the period of studies. For those who have a pre-existing illness on arrival, there may, however, be some doubt about how much of the treatment you can receive without cost. You need to check on this if it applies to you. Equally, if you are staying less than six months, you should try to ascertain what cover is provided for you. If it is inadequate, you may have to take out private health insurance. The standard of health care is generally very high in the UK and the 'free' coverage runs from medical consultations to major operations, if required (which thankfully for most students they are not). There are a few items, however, for which you may have to pay – such as a statutory price for prescriptions and for many aspects of dental treatment (other than check-ups). If you feel these are likely to mount up over time (something rather unlikely except for the vulnerable, perhaps), a small insurance policy could again be the answer.

POLICE REGISTRATION

Many of those arriving in the UK as students are required to register with the police. Instructions about this are put in your passport on arrival. Students from several countries, however, are not obliged to register: citizens of the European Economic Area, the USA, Japan and the countries of the Commonwealth are all exempt. There is nothing sinister about the process of registration. It is simply a means of officially recording a place of domicile for temporary residents in the UK. It must be done soon after arrival and in the city or town in which you are going to live. Changes of address also need to be recorded. In one sense police registration gives you recognition as a temporary citizen and to that extent offers you a degree of recognition and protection. But any form of compulsory registration can, inevitably, appear suspicious to some and it does cost money, which those required to register are obliged to pay.

SHOPPING AND EATING

The arrival of the supermarket has revolutionised shopping worldwide. It is now possible to buy goods almost without knowing one word of the local language. Most products on the shelves are also likely to be extremely familiar in appearance, even if brand names and labelling differ. The range of goods which can be obtained under one roof makes the whole process simpler and sometimes speedier, too. In time, perhaps, you may develop a more refined approach to shopping, which will take you into the specialist retailers. But initially the convenience of places which are usually open for longer hours than the specialist shops and which seem to stock all the necessities of life is likely to have a big allure. Without doubt you will be able to find there foods and other goods from many different countries and to suit many different tastes. If you don't find exactly what you are looking for, it is a good idea to make this known by a note to the manager. Many UK supermarkets in university areas are sensitive to the needs of the international student community and often stock goods, for example around Chinese New Year, for which there is predominantly a student demand.

One of the most urgent needs for new students is to try out the local food. If you develop a taste for it, it can involve a saving financially (local food is likely to be cheaper and more plentiful than more exotic foods) and it can help with your socialising. An early visit to the nearest student cafeteria is recommended (though that is not necessarily where British cooking is seen at its best!). Even if you find most local dishes to be entirely resistible, you are probably quite safe. The range of foods available in the UK is nowadays very large. British people travel widely and have developed a taste for food from many different countries. You may be surprised to discover that many locals now regard sushi, couscous, pizzas and tortillas as British food. In a large city, you can expect to find the ingredients for Chinese, Indian, Italian, French and Mexican cooking widely available in the shops. Certainly vegetarians are well catered for. Fruit, vegetables and spices from all over the world are also available (though some will cost more than the local equivalents). The current preference for light lunches has also led to a big expansion of sandwich bars and bistros. The UK also has specialist restaurants, of course, offering the cuisine of many different countries in the world, though some of those will be beyond the average student's budget except for special occasions. If you feel like cooking for yourself or expanding your repertoire as a cook, there are also numerous TV programmes and books available to encourage you further.

CONTACTING HOME

One thing regularly neglected by new arrivals is the need to contact home. Having survived the journey to the new institution, got through the orientation and embarked on the courses, students sometimes seem to feel that their success in this entitles them to a lengthy period of peace and quiet, or at least that is how it is perceived by many parents. It may be helpful to remind you that those who waved you goodbye will not have shared in your excitements and will be anxious to know what has become of you. A phone call, letter or e-mail about initial impressions goes down very well back home and may even help you to put the whole initial experience into perspective.

SOME QUESTIONS

When preparing to undertake a journey, what do you think needs to be kept uppermost in mind? Which of your possessions should you take along with you? What are your strategies for making new friends? Beyond your plans for studying in the UK, what are your longer-term academic and personal plans?

PART II
Study Skills

10   MAKING THE MOST OF YOUR STUDIES

GETTING STARTED

If orientation can sometimes seem like an embarrassment of riches, the start of term brings a welcome sense of order and method and a central return to what most students feel is their principal goal – studying. By that stage, the process of transition from one academic system to another is over and you are now securely launched on your new programme. Continuing the athletics metaphor of this series, you are no longer just set but are out of your blocks and into your stride. Being an international student has, of course, a great deal in common with being any other kind of student. But there are occasions when the international perspective has a particular significance. This chapter tries to offer a few tips for international students on making the most of academic studies in the UK.

Knowing yourself

Everyone is agreed that to get the most out of your life as a student, it is important to know yourself, to know why you are studying, what you hope to achieve by the studies and what they mean to you personally. International students are no different in this respect from locals. Some commentators suggest, however, that international students are distinguishable from home students by their circumstances. In most cases, international students will have travelled a lot further in search of education. They will almost certainly have invested more of their time in preparing for the transition. It is likely that they will have involved their families and friends more in their decision to undertake the studies. Many of them (and their families) will have made a much greater financial investment in the studies than domestic students have done. Some will be conscious, as scholarship holders, of the investment that others have made in them, the honour accorded them, the opportunity which they have been given. It is sometimes alleged that this tends to make many international students more goal-directed than domestic students, more ambitious sometimes, perhaps more anxious to succeed – and more afraid of failure.

None of this may be true of you, of course. You may view things entirely differently. But your reasons for undertaking the studies are still worth thinking about. If you are strongly committed or unusually anxious, this does not mean that you will not be successful. But it does mean that you will have to manage your drive or your anxiety. To do this requires that you should be aware of it and be able to allow for it when considering your progress. Being aware of why you are under-taking your studies also means being better able to see the studies in perspective. It is likely that you will have a great variety of motives for studying and that many of the factors involved will have more to do with you as a person than with the intrinsic appeal of the subject or with the fact that you were successful in examinations. Thinking things out can help you to become more focused and hopefully also more self-aware and so more objective. For most observers, this is a key part of settling down and of becoming more relaxed and confident in what you are doing. Once you've thought out why you are studying, you will still no doubt respect others who have a different perspective from you, but you won't feel that you need to follow them.

Being a student

In general, students in the UK live and study away from home. You may have travelled further but you won't essentially be in a different situation in this respect. One result of this is that it is the institution which now supplies or oversees those things which home had earlier provided – comfortable housing, secure social supports, concerned welfare, intellectual encouragement. In the UK, this new, different, more self-reliant environment produces a very strong sense of academic community. As a student, you rub shoulders every day with others who resemble you in age, ability and interests. You interact together in an atmosphere based on mutual respect and tolerance. You take on the different roles of being a 'student'. At its best, this is a life-enhancing experience and many individuals have testified to its liberating effects on them. It may be so for you from the start. But it can also be daunting to realise how much others seem to be gaining (and how quickly) especially if initially you feel tentative and uncertain about your own involvement, as many people do. Fortunately, confidence comes from experience as well as temperament. Knowing that it may take you some time to find your roles and make your full contribution can be helpful.

STUDY SKILLS

Learning new methods of studying at university and rehearsing old ones is something that all students find they have to do. It is part of the leap involved in moving from school to university or from undergraduate to postgraduate study. Since this is known and recognised, your lecturers are likely to offer instruction about methods which have proved effective in the past. Occasionally whole classes are devoted to this or provided outside normal class hours. If you have a course booklet, it is likely to be mentioned there, too. There are also now a large number of study skills books and pamphlets which can be read, designed to help you to come to terms with the skills involved. The series of books to which this one belongs all take this approach and relate their suggestions to particular academic disciplines. That is surely how study skills are best mastered since that is where the skills will be deployed. You should check the list at the front of this book to see which titles might be of use to you.

But it is also possible to think of study skills as applying to different groups. International students have a particular claim here. If you are operating in a second language, for example, you may be using skills which others are not. And if you have gained your earlier experience of study overseas, it makes sense to spend a little time ensuring that your experience of study at home has equipped you fully to meet the expectations of study which prevail in the UK. The likelihood is that some differences in teaching styles will be encountered and some new learning strategies will have to be considered. Again international students do not really face a different problem in this respect than home students – everyone goes through a period of adjustment. But in tackling it, you are occasionally confronted by an extra element, which relates to cultural expectations and practices.

Culture shock

Culture shock is normally provoked not when something is self-evidently different (as is often supposed) but rather when what appears to be the same turns out to be different. If, for example, you are in the habit of interrupting at lectures by asking the lecturer questions, you may be puzzled to be told to keep your questions till the end. Alternatively, if you expect always to have to keep silent, you may be surprised to be asked to respond to a question addressed directly to you. If you are used to writing an essay based on what you have been told in lectures and incorporating into it word-for-word excerpts from the recommended reading list, you may be even more astonished to be told that you are being unoriginal and are guilty of plagiarism. In these cases the confusion derives from simply assuming that a familiar form (a lecture, an essay) will always have the same underlying rules. It may do, but it may not. Different styles of teaching and different expectations of the learner operate between countries and within a country. Fortunately, instances of real culture shock are rare and usually occur seriously only once. Those who experience them seem to get inoculated by their first awareness of difference and thereafter adapt to local ways quite readily.

STUDY CYCLES

International students often experience a series of different responses in their reaction to the education system in the UK, sometimes coming all at once, sometimes in succession. The first is often elation, the excitement generated when everything seems new and positive and different. The second is a sharp reaction to this, when the realities of difference become problematic, alienating and unwelcome. It is when this negative response dominates that you are also likely to miss home and its familiar comforts most. But these phases are usually followed by a more balanced response when you see things more objectively and feel able to assess the strengths and weaknesses in the British system more dispassionately. Many educational authorities suggest that all study programmes, for domestic and well as international students, follow a similar cycle. They feel that we often progress through interest and enthusiasm to puzzlement and cynicism before a balanced appreciation and deeper understanding finally dawns. Knowing that you may experience some of these different responses can prepare you better to deal with them. It probably doesn't allow you to escape them all entirely. But it may indicate to you that what you are feeling is more widely shared and can be openly discussed with other students and your advisers.

THE STUDY ROUTINE

For undergraduates and taught postgraduates, one of the most important study skills you will need to master is establishing a work routine. Without it, study is much harder. The UK's education system expects students to develop this routine on their own. If that sounds unfamiliar to you, you must give it some thought. You will find that you are left with a significant amount of time during the day and also in the evening when you do not have to attend classes, but no clear indication of how this time must be spent. If you are to succeed in your studies, you will have to develop a work routine whereby this 'free time' is used productively. Such a routine is not easily achieved and most students find it takes some effort and some application to get it right. Probably the best way to begin to deal with it is by drawing up a timetable for each hour and each day of the week and then make a determined effort to stick to the programme you design for yourself.

The timetable

There are a number of clear signposts which help you to establish your work pattern or routine. Each course is likely to have formal classes, lectures and tutorials and perhaps practicals each week. Attending these, though this may not always be a requirement, should be thought of as a fixed commitment initially. But, of course, more is expected of you than this. If you are to benefit fully from the course and to be successful, studying on your own outside classes is of central importance. This private element is likely to grow as your studies become more advanced. It is a particular feature of senior undergraduate and taught postgraduate work.

Most students find it difficult at first to develop a work routine for the private or personal side of studying. One essential problem is that of knowing how much time to allocate in total and then to ensure that sufficient time has been allowed for everything which needs to be included. This is where the timetable comes in. You have to block out all the times in the week when you have fixed activities to undertake. This will include your lectures and tutorials but also social activities, such as sports or societies or whatever other forms of extramural interest you favour. Obviously time for such necessities as eating and sleeping has to feature, too. It is also important that you build into this timetable some time for resting and relaxing. No one could or should study non-stop all day long.

You then need to decide how much private study time you are left with and how much you will need. You must assign time for each of the subjects you are undertaking (or for the different parts of the subject, if there is only one). Once all is settled, you have to make an effort to follow this programme, at least over the first few weeks. It can then be adjusted, as experience reveals what is best and as the work demands on you (essays, examinations) and perhaps social demands (which can also vary) wax and wane. Eventually, by being performed regularly and routinely, the work comes to involve a great deal less effort and hopefully develops its own interest and enjoyment.

UK ATTITUDES

In talking about your private study to British students, you need to be aware of one cultural peculiarity. In the UK, students like to give the impression that they do very little private work. They don't want to appear to be a 'swot' (a person who neglects his or her friends by spending too much time studying, a character commonly found in public school literature of the nineteenth century). Effortless academic ability is what is apparently prized most. It is important to grasp, however, that this concept exists only in fiction. Every student does work privately at university and those whose interests are strongly engaged or who are keen to do well will work very hard indeed. You should certainly expect to spend a good deal of time in private study and to give this no less consideration than you give to public commitments like lectures or tutorials. Much of it, no doubt, will be spent on undertaking required work – like essays or projects or examination preparation – but some of it will be genuinely independent study in which you are pursuing your own interests and enthusiasms within the course, refining your opinions and gaining in personal understanding. If you also develop the habit of making light of this work when talking to your fellow students, you will begin to realise with some embarrassment that you are becoming more British than the British!

CLASSWORK: TEACHING METHODS

It isn't easy to define the different kinds of classes which you are likely to meet. So much is dependent on your choice of discipline and even on the policies and practices of your institution. Studies in fine art and in mathematics do not use precisely the same methods of instruction as studies in politics or languages. But it is highly likely for everyone, except perhaps research students, that your course will involve a significant number of lectures. For these, of course, you will be sitting in a large room with many other students listening to a speaker. Being a listener is not the only role you can or should play. It used to be the case in the UK that students never interrupted during a lecture to ask questions, though in recent times lecturing styles have become more varied and some lecturers positively invite this. Every lecturer, whatever style is employed, usually allows time at the end of lectures when she or he will remain at the podium to provide you with the opportunity to clarify matters or make points individually. Lecturers also allocate other times in the week when you can see them privately, if there are matters in the lectures you would like to discuss further. You can also see them by special appointment if those times don't suit.

It is likely that your classes will also include tutorials or practicals, in which the large lecture class is divided up into small discussion or work groups, involving perhaps only a few students and a tutor or demonstrator. This is another chance for you to have your say on the topics being explored. Many senior and postgraduate classes make much use of yet another format, **seminars**, which resemble tutorials in involving group discussions but are usually much larger. Seminars are often led off by a short oral presentation by one or a number of students each time (a technique also used in many tutorials). Tutors and seminar organisers, like lecturers, are also usually available if you would like to see them privately. You therefore have several opportunities to follow things up and should feel free to do so.

Learning from lectures

Virtually all undergraduate and taught postgraduate students spend a huge amount of time sitting in lectures, usually making copious notes. Some never refer to the notes again and soon have forgotten the lectures. This is certainly not the most productive use of anyone's time. If you feel you do this, there are ways you can try to make your listening and note-taking more productive. Each lecturer has an individual style and you may find that you have to get used to this. Some talk rapidly, some slowly. Some are easily understood, some less so. Some use lists and number their points as they go along. Others use an entirely discursive approach, leaving it up to you to decide where the breaks in the material lie. Attending lectures is one way of gaining experience of different forms of English academic discourse. Lectures illustrate the different ways in which academics form and present arguments and deploy evidence in their support. Listened to actively in this way, you will find that they offer a good deal, whatever the quality of your notes.

But lectures, of course, are expected to do much more than that. Beyond the mechanics of their delivery, you also have to concentrate on what is said. Lectures set out the parameters of the course, indicating what material you are expected to cover. They outline the principal topics which are being covered and the different ways in which these topics are to be addressed. Since any subject is likely to be virtually limitless, an indication of what you need to know about and what you need not know about is particularly helpful. Virtually all lectures succeed in communicating that. They may do more by making the material relevant to your previous knowledge or experience. Lectures are also supposed to inspire and at their best they may do that, too. If so, a subject which you may earlier have thought of as dull or difficult becomes suddenly fascinating. Unfortunately, few lectures are quite as compelling as that. But it is probably best to persist with even a difficult lecturer until you are sure that the experience is not productive.

Taking notes at lectures

Many international students say that they find it is difficult to listen to a lecture and take notes at the same time. More disappointingly still, even if you were to succeed in doing this effectively and then in repeating what you've noted down in an examination, it would probably not be enormously well received. One famous joke defines a lecture as a process of transmitting information from the lecturer's script to the student's notebook without it passing through the minds of either party. The joke is meant to show that the real purpose of listening to (and delivering) a lecture is not just to record but to think about what is being communicated. By the time you are required to write about the subject in essays or examinations, you are expected to have considered it sufficiently for you to be able to put everything you have heard into your own words and to display your own knowledge and understanding of the subject. That process is best begun in the lecture itself. You need to have a note of what material was covered. But it is infinitely better in trying to record the content to attempt summaries of the major points (which requires thought) rather than seeking to capture a few words of every sentence (which doesn't). As with most things in life, this doesn't come easily, but practice makes perfect. It is also important rapidly to read over your notes soon afterwards to ensure that they make sense and accurately convey the impression you retain of what was said.

Lectures and reading

You are expected to do some background reading to assist with your understanding of lectures and again this is likely to grow the more advanced you get in your studies. Lecturers usually indicate which works they think would be most valuable for this purpose (it may be simply a recommended textbook for the course) or they point you towards hand-outs or class books or even particular sections within the library which contain the information they recommend. This is particularly helpful when the lecture has inspired you to find out more about the subject or when the lecture has left you unclear about what was being said. It provides a means for you to step back and consolidate your knowledge, so that you never find yourself lost or unable to follow new material. But students tend not to attempt to supplement every lecture in this way since the effort could be quite overwhelming. The main purpose of reading in order to support lectures is to develop a surer grasp of the material, something which is often aided by having more than one source of opinion to consider and more than one set of evidence to examine. But it is not aided by getting lost in the detail. Concentrating on what you feel you understand best and find most interesting and also what the lecturers say are the most important topics is what most students do.

CLASSWORK: TUTORIALS

The tutorials can be helpful in a different way to lectures though they too often serve as signposts. In a tutorial, students are expected to discuss a pre-arranged topic with each other and with the tutor. As the subjects under discussion form themes in the course, you are again gaining an understanding of the parameters as well as of the content of the course. But in a tutorial you are also interrogating (or being interrogated by) the tutor and your fellow students and discovering how far your understanding of the material covered matches theirs. Tutorials also enable you to gain some understanding of the complexity of knowledge. You come to appreciate the genuine differences of opinion that are possible, for example, even amongst those who agree on 'the facts', the data or the evidence. This emphasis on the diversity of opinion, on the tentativeness of academic knowledge, is not found in all educational styles, and even in the UK may be more a feature of advanced classes than elementary ones. But it is none the less a fundamental part of British higher education and it is wise to give it some attention.

Tutorials only work well if all students in the class do some preparation for them, in order to ensure that everyone has a basic grasp of the subject under discussion. If you are going to be able to do this and to form your own point of view, you will have to allocate time to do the necessary preparatory reading. Tutorials also demand that you should be prepared to venture an opinion in class, when appropriate, even if this means leaving yourself open to criticism. That can be difficult for some international students or at least for those who are operating in a second language and are not confident of their ability in argument. But it is also a concern initially for other students, too. You need to remember that tutorials are open-ended discussions, not finals examination papers. What is important is that you should participate in the discussion, not that you should have developed fully formed, impregnable arguments. The tutors are hoping you will use the tutorial to try out ideas which appeal to you. There is no problem if you later discard those ideas, having decided that they lack substance or conviction.

Social learning opportunities

Tutorials and laboratory classes provide opportunities for you to make friends easily by bringing you into regular contact with other students in the class and requiring you all to discuss things together. It is a good idea to build on this. If after the class you invite one or two of the others to go for coffee or tea, you can continue your discussion there. It is then easy to move on to discuss studies generally and how you are finding the lectures and other classes. Sharing your impressions in this way is enormously helpful. It reveals how much you have in common with other students and that your concerns are theirs too. It allows you to be open and frank about things you might not wish to mention in the more formal setting of a class. It helps you to begin to feel a member of the group, especially when you get on to the topic of the shortcomings of the lecturers or the weaknesses in the lectures!

TAUGHT MASTER'S

Taught master's students face a particular kind of challenge in their studies. Master's courses are 'intensive'. Almost from the first day you are expected to be able to follow lectures, participate in tutorials and seminars and plan for your course work project. But it helps that you are likely to be much more mature (well, certainly older!) than most undergraduates and you will have a much more varied set of experiences of studying and learning behind you. This generally makes it easier for you to get together with others in the class to discuss matters. It also allows you to be more assertive about requiring explicit directions from the academic staff about your work requirements. If this is your first time of studying in the UK, you should think of doing both. Even if you are not invited to, you can take an early opportunity to suggest social get-togethers of the class and to arrange for class spokespersons to be nominated to negotiate further with the tutors. You do need to be very clear from the start (and throughout the whole course) about what is expected of you and what you can expect of your tutors. Formal and informal opportunities to discuss these requirements outside class are one way to achieve this. Taught master's courses represent a bridge to research work and therefore emphasise independent and group learning far more than undergraduate courses do. This puts a premium on being clear about goals and targets and knowing when and where you can obtain feedback on your progress.

SOME QUESTIONS

Many universities organise study skills sessions for new students. What would you hope to learn from these? Having decided where you would like further help, from what sources other than study skills sessions would you look for assistance?

11 USING YOUR FREE STUDY TIME

READING AND PRIVATE STUDY

University students in the UK are all expected to do independent reading. For undergraduates and taught postgraduates, as mentioned, this is sometimes in order to consolidate or deepen understanding of a subject first broached in lectures. Sometimes the reading is undertaken independently to gain a more rounded or more detailed understanding of one of the topics on the course. Sometimes it is used to search out information which will be required for a tutorial or seminar or in preparation for an essay or examination. Sometimes it is simply to allow you to pursue your own interests, to find out more about some subject which you believe to be of value to you. For many courses, a textbook or perhaps textbooks will be recommended, and these (particularly when you have been persuaded to purchase them) are often used as a primary source of information for all these purposes. But a textbook will not be enough to cover all your reading requirements and you will have to range more widely still. Most courses have not only recommended course books but also detailed reading lists, setting out extensive suggestions for further reading, all of which will be in the university library. It is important to realise that these are not meant as an indication of the work which you are expected to perform. You are not normally required to have read everything on a reading list and it would be rather unwise even to try to do so unless this is explicitly recommended. The expectation is more likely to be that in your studies you may at some time feel a need to look for further information (for some of the many reasons given earlier). With these lists, you will easily be able to identify relevant books and articles which your tutors judge to be useful and reliable, rather than having to roam around the library hoping to spot something of value.

Note-taking from books

Making notes from books, like making notes at lectures, is another skill which for many of us needs to be worked on and mastered. The advice you are most often given in the UK, perhaps with an intention to shock, is never to read an academic book from cover to cover. Instead you are encouraged to treat books as a resource and to extract from them only what you need for your purposes. That probably means beginning with the table of contents and index, to find what the book seems to be about. Once you've flicked through the work and identified which sections seem most likely to be helpful, you then have to decide what coverage to give them. Do you skim read (another area where practice certainly helps) or read assiduously? In making notes, you will want to record an indication of the likely interest of the work for your purposes. You will also need notes on those arguments or points of view in the book which relate to your topic and some indication of the evidence on which these viewpoints are based. As with taking notes at lectures, summaries which require you to think about what you have read, expressed in your own words, are infinitely to be preferred to verbatim extracts. But a few excerpts from the book, phrases or sentences which seem to sum up an argument or which precisely capture a piece of evidence, can be valuable. You may be able to employ them later as a means of enlivening your text when you come to use your notes in an essay or for an examination. To avoid the danger of plagiarism (discussed later in this chapter), you should try always to keep a full record of the sources from which you have made your notes or copied down quotations. This can save a great deal of time when at a later stage you come to prepare your assessed work.

ASSESSED WORK

You will probably spend more of your private study time preparing essays, reports or papers, writing up projects and revising for examinations than undertaking any of the other private study activities which have been mentioned. This is largely because these are the elements which are normally assessed and often count towards your degree result. Most students, very sensibly, give more time to work which is assessed than to work which is not assessed. Unassessed work is still extremely valuable. It allows you to take chances, to try out ideas, to experiment with different approaches, to gain insights which you will later deploy in work which may be assessed. You need to do that if you are to make progress in studying. But assessed work is likely to concentrate the mind more. There is no rule in the UK about the amount of work which will be assessed, and practice is likely to vary between institutions and between subjects. This, of course, makes it vital for you to know whenever you join a class what the rules are on assessment. In general, however, the UK assesses only a relatively small number of projects in each course. This is partly explained by the belief that originality is best encouraged by giving you space in which to learn for yourself. If your progress in the course is examined very frequently, you will tend simply to repeat what your lecturers have said in class since there is no time for anything else. If you are assessed less, it is thought, you become freer to pursue your own researches and to reach your own conclusions. But this, of course, then makes the elements which are assessed, the essays, reports and examinations, extremely important.

Preparing an essay or paper

Most students are familiar with essay-writing before they go to university. The main differences initially appear to be that the book lists lengthen, the libraries are much bigger and more complex in arrangement and the time allowed for completion of the project is often greater. You usually have to be selective amongst the reading and need to ask yourself which works are likely to be most useful. But you may also have to find your own way to the sources, with only the topic and the arrangement of the library to guide you. There are sometimes differences, too, in what is expected of you in writing an essay which again may make the familiar form unfamiliar. In universities in the UK what is sought is usually a carefully assembled argument which directly addresses the question and supplies a considered response to it. Though the argument has to consist of your thoughts on the question asked, it will be based on and will display an awareness of the views which the leading authors have expressed in the books and articles available to you. It will also make clear the grounds on which these views are held and may mention any reservations which have been expressed about them. Essays which simply discuss each of the books on the reading list in turn, summarising the views and evidence they contain without addressing the question more closely, are much less highly prized. Again, developing and presenting an argument in this way is something that you may have to try out many times before you feel you are getting it right.

Plagiarism

Plagiarism can create confusion for students. You are expected to know the views of the authors of the books you read. It is hoped that you will make notes from their books and use them in writing your essays. If, however, you quote from someone else's work directly in your essay without attributing the quotation to its source, you can be accused of plagiarism and severely penalised. This is sometimes hard to understand. What is wrong with using material which is in the public domain? The explanation relates fundamentally to academic cultural norms. Authors' words and ideas are regarded as their own property. Even if you feel what you read precisely answers the question you are asked, you cannot use their words without acknowledgement. Doing so is almost like copying the work of another student. To give appropriate acknowledgement, you may need to use quotation marks and to cite the author and book title either in the text or in a footnote. It also helps if you add a phrase or sentence to explain why you have quoted them. If you are borrowing ideas, you actually strengthen your work by acknowledging your source. It is then clear that you are able to use the work of an established scholar in support of an argument which you have assembled, something that suggests a real understanding and must inevitably carry a good deal of weight.

Preparing for an examination

Examinations are seldom popular, particularly those ones which test knowledge over the entire course of study and form a central part of the assessment. Students who clearly see such exams as of equal significance to the day of creation sometimes call them 'big bang' exams. Those writing in a second language often feel disadvantaged by them since they are time-limited and rapidity of thought and expression seems to be a major requirement (though good preparation can help here). Actually, total 'big bangs' are now comparatively rare in the UK where 'continuous assessment' (which allows class work projects taken throughout the year to count as a pro-portion of the total assessment) is much more the norm. But you are likely to encounter several important examinations and have to be prepared for them. To overcome any anxiety, what you most need is to be prepared. It is important, for example, that you should know the format which is being used and the numbers of questions and the kinds of question that are likely to be asked. It helps even more to begin by looking at past papers (they are usually available in the university li-brary). And you should try as part of your preparation to complete one exam paper on your own, doing the whole thing in real time, as this can inspire confidence and/or reveal what more you need to do to be even more fully prepared.

Preparing for an exam is a matter of maximising your assets. You will have already done a good deal of work during the course on class work, essays, projects, tutorial preparation and private reading. If you begin with what you feel you have already covered and what you feel you understand well, the task suddenly seems less daunting. Of course, you will have to revise what you know so that it is fresh in your mind. This means active re-learning: not just reading over your notes but re-summarising them or trying to express the things you've mastered in different ways. Beyond this, you have to be guided by your experience. Most students feel it is necessary to 'spot' questions, to anticipate what topics are likely to arise. This is a perfectly sensible strategy, provided that you make your choice sufficiently broad and don't concentrate entirely on the more peripheral topics. There is also a danger in lopsided revision, giving too much attention to a very few congenial subjects to the neglect of more obvious ones. Evidently you must have prepared at least as many topics as you will have to answer questions on, and most people would suggest that one or two more are needed for safety. After all, the question can defeat you even when the topic is one you've covered. But once you are prepared, you should try to look forward to the exam as an opportunity for you to capitalise on the work you've done.

Sitting an examination

There are certain obvious points about sitting an examination which are often neglected. Firstly, you must be able to find the examination hall. This means checking where the examination will be held and finding out how to get there and how long this takes. Secondly, you have to arrive in good time. That will mean checking the starting time and perhaps also setting your alarm (you can use two if necessary) to ensure that you depart promptly. Thirdly, you have to remember to bring along anything needed for the exam (like pens or a watch, for example). You might make a list and put this somewhere prominent (on your door?) to remind yourself. With all that done, you have good prospects of arriving comfortable and cheerful. If for any reason you are unable to attend the exam, you must inform someone in authority (the course director, your tutor?) as soon as possible. When illness is the cause, you need to get a medical certificate and report also that you have it.

Writing an examination

Students seldom fail an exam because they know too little. They mainly fail because they 'ran out of time' or 'misread the question' or 'got bogged down'. Timing is terribly important. You have to apportion the time you are allowed carefully. Ideally, a short time at the beginning needs to be devoted to carefully reading the instructions and all the questions, giving them thought before deciding which ones you will tackle. Remember that the instructions can be different from those in the last examination paper you sat and that a question can initially appear to cover unfamiliar material and yet on reflection be straightforward. The bulk of the time has to be divided amongst the number of questions you are required to answer. If all questions are weighted equally, you may want to allow slightly more time for your best ones and slightly less for the one you will do last. It cannot be strikingly less, however, as not being able to get to your last question can be disastrous. If you feel examination nerves are affecting you, you may also want to allow a little time to read over the paper at the end. In order to do all this well, you probably have to rehearse it in advance. It helps if you also write down (and subsequently score out) what you expect to be the precise times at which you will move from one activity or one question to the next. You must then stick to your timings. It requires courage to spend time on planning during an exam. Sometimes you get the feeling that your neighbours have embarked on their third answer before you've got into your first.

OBTAINING FEEDBACK FROM TUTORS

Essays, projects and examinations are often marked and returned to you with extensive comments, both written and verbal, by the tutor. Every tutor knows that what a student usually does on such occasions is to look immediately at the mark or assessment, to glance over or listen defensively to the comments and then to put the piece away. Only once the pressure of an end-of-course examination provides a compelling reason will it be looked at again. Arguably, that is to make very poor use of a valuable resource, the tutor's considered opinion. Tutors see their role in two ways. In assessment, they will be deciding on a mark or a value to be attached to the work performed. This is obviously important in terms of passing and failing or gaining distinction. But it is probably the aspect of the work of a tutor that most of them find least congenial. In attaching comments, however, tutors are doing what they feel they do best – encouraging students to learn. They are not trying to trip you up or to fail you. They are trying to decide what you were aiming at in your work and then to provide you with help which will enable you to come closer to achieving your aim next time.

If you are going to benefit from this, you have to spend some time going over the comments and asking yourself what point your tutor is making. It is important that you should look not just for why, in the tutor's opinion, you appeared to go wrong, but also why you got it right. Criticism is mainly about trying to make the acceptable into the good, not about berating the incompetent. If you feel uncertain about that or suspect that your work has been misunderstood, it is quite normal to ask to see the tutor privately to talk over your concerns. What you have to try and avoid is the feeling that any criticism is hurtful and that it is easier to cope by ignoring all critical comments. That attitude places a very low estimation on your capacity to improve and on the university teacher's capacity to help you do so. It is much more rewarding for both of you if you find you have to ask your tutor to explain something further rather than decide that the tutor's comments are best treated by being entirely ignored.

Obtaining feedback from friends

Another much neglected source of assistance is the work of fellow students. There is no reason why you should not ask your friends and colleagues how they are doing on the course. Talking things over with fellow students, which is, of course, a central part of tutorials, can be just as valuable when done for other areas of study. You may even decide to exchange essays or written work. Sometimes it is easier to learn by seeing what others have done which has been well received rather than by trying to learn from one's own experience. Students are all in the same boat. They have undergone much the same instruction, been set similar goals and probably share an equal enthusiasm for the subject. To see what one of your fellow students has achieved from the same starting point can be quite enlightening. Sharing one's understanding with others can also build a greater mutual confidence, improve class discussions and create the basis for working co-operatively, something that is of value far beyond the classroom. Some tutors tell students that they learn more from each other in the coffee room than they do from attending classes. That can be put down to academic modesty, real or affected, in part. But there's certainly some truth in it, too.

SOME QUESTIONS

When you are writing an essay, what are the stages by which you begin to form an argument? In your discipline, how do you distinguish argument from evidence? Using a short article which you admire, try to analyse the structure by setting out, briefly, the main argument, the principal subsidiary points and the nature of the evidence used.

12 RESEARCH STUDY

RESEARCH SKILLS

Research students often have to deploy different study skills from undergraduates and taught postgraduates (though research projects are part of nearly all degrees). It is difficult to generalise about the needs of research, given the diversity of subjects in which research is conducted and the different practices which prevail in different institutions. There has also been a movement away from 'pure research degrees' in the UK towards more diverse research training programmes. The skills research postgraduates require today probably encompass all those already considered as typical of taught programmes. But the dominant element is still independent research and this makes for a form of study with its own rather special needs. It deserves a separate chapter.

TAUGHT ELEMENTS

Research students usually work mainly on their own and attend far fewer lectures and tutorials than taught course students. Historically, UK research degrees were almost entirely performed individually. The students worked alone (even if sometimes as part of a larger team) on a research project agreed with their supervisors. Of course repeated consultations between student and supervisor were required. Today, taught course elements are more and more likely to be part of the work of every research student, certainly at the start of the research project (when generic training programmes are held) and often beyond that. In the new degree combining research with a large amount of 'course work', which a small group of universities in the UK has recently introduced, the period of study has been extended to accommodate this. In other cases, the taught elements are incorporated into the minimum period. And you will still find examples of programmes which involve little or no course work. You need to check, therefore, which model will apply to you.

Course work elements have been introduced to provide more guidance on methodology and to bring in broader thematic or more general or applied studies. The idea is to make sure that the research project, which has to be sharply focused, is also seen in a wider context. This is also sometimes held to broaden the degree's usefulness and to give it extra vocational value. The same or a similar idea lies behind a move to encourage all doctoral students first to undertake a master's degree. Traditionally in the UK the able student was allowed to move directly from undergraduate studies to doctoral studies. In recent years, a master's degree (particularly the research master's and those master's which contain a strong element of both taught work and research work) is often recommended – and sometimes required – for anyone thinking of doing research. The master's then forms a secure bridge between the two. Students become better prepared to pursue their advanced work. They are made more aware of the nature and pressures of independent research before they decide to embark on the lengthy process of undertaking a doctoral programme. This can, of course, also persuade some to settle for the intermediate degree. Those who go on beyond the master's are likely to be quite highly motivated.

SUPERVISION

The supervisor – student relationship is always going to be at the heart of research work. Getting this relationship right is the major task that all research students face. Supervisors usually have a multitude of responsibilities and may have many commitments which take up a great deal of their time. Some supervisors arrange to see you on a regular basis at fixed times.

This is helpful in ensuring you access, but it will require you to keep a note of the problems you encounter and the issues you want to discuss when you meet. Even if you have little to discuss, you should keep the appointments. Research work is distinctly isolating, and meeting someone with an informed interest in your work on a regular basis has social and psychological as well as academic benefits. Other supervisors prefer to set you some task and then ask you to report after an appropriate period to discuss how you have performed. This means that the task determines the intervals between your meetings, which can be unhelpful, but does give you assured access and a focus for your discussions. Still other supervisors leave it to you to suggest when to meet (though they are likely to complain eventually if you keep your distance). This allows you to get help at the time you feel it is most needed, but imposes on you the obligation of deciding both when that is required and what needs to be discussed. If you can influence the method of supervision to be used, it is wise to have your say and to agree it in advance what suits you both best.

Occasionally, the relationship between the student and the supervisor is difficult to manage. Being an apprentice, as research students are, trying to learn from a supervisor but also to establish yourself as a fully professional scholar, is not simple. You can feel aggrieved with your supervisor for a variety of perfectly understandable reasons. Some students and supervisors are able to talk this over and sort it out, which is ideal. Everyone should at least try that first. In some cases, however, it does prove hard. Your institution may well have anticipated this and provided mechanisms for you to make the problems known. In many cases, for example, you are allocated two supervisors and are encouraged to approach either as required. No one likes to complain; however this opportunity to talk things over with a relatively independent second opinion can be beneficial. In other cases, the research unit in which you are working may have appointed an individual to serve as the head of unit or the adviser to postgraduate students. If so, you can approach that person to discuss matters in confidence. The growth of research schools in the UK (another marked development of recent times) has been distinctly helpful in this respect. You can also seek help in the wider area of student welfare, from student counsellors, for example. The one thing you must not do is to sit and suffer in silence. This relationship has to work for you to succeed and you have to ensure that it does. That is not to imply, of course, that you should anticipate that you will always find it difficult to remain on good terms with your supervisor. It is only to emphasise that relationships need to be worked at, including professional ones, and that they change over time.

THE RESEARCH PROPOSAL

Finding a precise topic for research almost always involves a dialogue with your supervisor and sometimes with other scholars, too. The necessity of producing something original, of working at the educational frontier, means inevitably that the choice of topic also has to be somewhat tentative and has to leave room for adjustments as the research proceeds and unexpected avenues open up. It is also likely that you will initially be severely dependent on your supervisor's opinions since you are unlikely to know the whole range of the research completed (though not necessarily published) and in progress. You can, however, do your best to survey the recent literature in books and journals. Even so, the unwelcome discovery some time into your research that someone else elsewhere is working on the same topic can drive you to have to change your topic altogether. More likely it will require some changes in your approach. On the other hand, it is unwise to agree any project with your supervisor which doesn't from the beginning have a real interest for you. Motivation is an issue for nearly all research students. Few maintain their enthusiasm un-dimmed throughout all the years of study. You must at least start by seeing value and interest in what you propose to undertake.

HOME AND AWAY

Sometimes you will want your research to reflect or be concerned with a topic of major interest to your own country. It
may well be necessary in consequence to collect data or to
undertake experiments at home. Topics of this kind are
particularly encouraged by a number of funding bodies and
governments in developing countries. They argue that much
research in the developed world trains students to work
mainly in a developed economy, rather than in their own.
The fear is that students, on graduation, will look for jobs in
the North and a brain drain will result. To avoid this, many
universities will make provision for you to spend time abroad
as part of your studies. They will also do this if you need to
collect research data abroad as an aspect of your project. But
when part of the study has to be undertaken abroad, there will
usually be a requirement that you must be able to stay in close
touch with your supervisors – by e-mail, fax, letter or even
video-conferencing – while you are away. The rules often
specify that your supervisor must visit you on site in order
to ensure that your research is proceeding satisfactorily. There
may be a requirement that a local supervisor must be appointed to substitute for the UK one temporarily. There will
certainly be some rules on the minimum amount of time that
you must remain in the UK. Whatever is agreed, these 'home
and away' arrangements are seldom lax. They are sometimes
seen by students as a way of cutting costs (by allowing you to
live more cheaply at home or to save on fees) but they can in
fact involve extra expenses and so prove financially neutral. If
you intend to do some of your research abroad, it is important
to check on the rules which operate and on their financial
implications.

STUDY SKILLS FOR RESEARCH STUDENTS

Because research methodology is so much dependent on the
discipline and is constantly being advanced, study skills books

for research students tend to be less plentiful than for taught course students. But they are there and you should certainly read at least one of them. They normally spend a good deal of time emphasising the importance of time management. There are good reasons for this. Research students have a tendency to be over-ambitious and to over-run their time limit. Quite a number fail to complete the doctoral thesis within three years, the normal prescribed minimum period. In recent years, this has led to understandable complaints from the sponsoring authorities who feel that they are being driven into supplying supplementary funding which they had not anticipated and, as a result, being denied opportunities to fund others. To tackle the problem, you need to bear two things firmly in mind. Firstly, you are undertaking work which requires you to demonstrate that you have mastered the skills which your discipline involves. This does not require you to re-invent the discipline. You must show competence. But that can be demonstrated in even a modest project. Secondly, you need a project which makes allowance for your time constraints. You should agree with your supervisor some proposal that is considered 'manageable' within the minimum time you are allowed. The project will develop and alter as you progress and you need to be able to adapt to that. But you must make sure that the changes you make are not luring you into waters which are too deep (a matter for discussion with your supervisor). And you need to keep looking out for the moment when you can say that your data-collection and analysis is sufficient and it is time to begin to head for home (or at least to complete the first draft). This is often a frustrating moment as you realise how much more there is to be known. But there will be time for more comprehensive coverage, hopefully, once the thesis is out of the way.

Setting deadlines

One crucial element in conducting research is the setting of deadlines. Some students embark on their research as an almost limitless exercise, conscious that the submission date is perhaps three years away and that a dazzlingly vast expanse of research material is immediately opening up before them. That way lies frustration. It is much better to decide from the beginning that you will provide your supervisor at regular intervals with a piece of written work. In the initial stages, this could be a description and analysis of what is already known about your chosen subject. As you get into your research data, it is more likely to be a preliminary study of initial findings – particularly those which seem to fit together and form a coherent body of evidence. Later, it might even take the form of a possible conference paper. It doesn't matter if none of these papers will appear as chapters in the final thesis. They will all move you forward to the point where your 'thesis', your contribution to the subject, is beginning to form. There is a great temptation not to do this initially. You are aware how little ground you have travelled and how much there is to know. But the temptation needs to be resisted. The goal can only be reached by marking out mileposts along the way. The written work is also the way in which your supervisor will become most clearly aware of your research and of its potential. Writing things down and presenting them at regular intervals also allows the supervisor to offer guidance and advice at crucial stages in the work's development.

At each stage (certainly at the end of every year, occasionally more frequently) your supervisor will be required to report on your progress to the postgraduate board and perhaps to your sponsors. Your written work will form a strong element in this report. Supervisors are aware of the various stages through which students go on the way to completion. They are not expecting evidence of outstanding originality or powerful insights at the report stage – or indeed at any stage perhaps. Instead they are hoping for evidence that you are getting through a body of work which is moving you towards a successful demonstration of your aptitude in the discipline. They may be able to observe that you are making progress or they may pick it up from discussions with you. But the crucial evidence will be what you submit. If you submit only one piece of work, near a deadline, it will become a real effort for you. If you have agreed earlier deadlines and taken on less comprehensive tasks, the effort is correspondingly more manageable.

GET A LIFE

In order to be successful, your research has to make a contribution to scholarship. By definition that means that you are often working on a project about which others know little. You yourself may not be entirely convinced of its value and significance until it is virtually complete. This makes research work quite testing of your commitment and dedication. Alternatively, you may be so obsessed with it that you can talk of nothing else, which will be testing of your social relationships. If, as often happens, your research requires you to be alone with your materials over lengthy periods, it can test your reserves of character too. For all these reasons, it is wise to have strategies which remind you that you are not alone. The research unit may arrange postgraduate seminars. If so, it helps to attend them, and to use them to make friends. If none exist or if they meet only occasionally, you can get together with other like-minded students to establish a regular seminar where you can read papers to each other and discuss them. Sometimes groups of students from one country or one area of the world will form a discussion group. This typically centres on the research you are all doing (it can be very revealing to discover how research is conducted in different fields of study). You can also invite visitors to speak to the group, perhaps those with an interest in your country or in internationalism. Or you can arrange extramural social events, particularly when families or partners are involved. More than most, research students need to know that they have a life outside the laboratory or library and that this needs cultivating, too.

COMPLETING

Most authorities are agreed that it is easy to over-estimate and under-estimate the amount of work required for a research degree. The recommended time limit is one known guideline which should help in this respect. There are others. The regulations governing completion and submission of theses and dissertations are almost invariably published and available for students to consult. Many students don't do so until they are well advanced in their research. The regulations are likely to be too bland and general to serve as guides to what is required in your research (you have to look to your supervisor and your own reading of books, articles and dissertations for that) but they may make clear a number of key issues. Many of them, for example, define what standards you are expected to reach. Many use the term 'an original contribution to scholarship' as a requirement of dissertations. Some go further and suggest what 'an original contribution' might be. Some even provide a definition for 'a thesis' ('a coherent argument', 'a new distillation of previously uncollected materials' and so on). That can be helpful to you in planning and directing your research and in shaping your analyses. Almost all prescribe a length for the submitted work which, when apportioned to chapters, may indicate how much material you are going to be able to include. These are useful pointers when read at an early stage in the research process and potentially alarming surprises when discovered near the end.

Writing up

Leaving sufficient time for the writing up of your research is another issue which must be faced. If you have been progressing systematically, some of the writing should have begun long before the gathering of the data is complete. Theses, like all other literary products, usually have to be re-written several times before they approach anything like completion. There is a skill to expressing yourself succinctly, powerfully and well, a skill to deploying your material to maximum effect, a skill to connecting the pieces into a coherent whole. These skills all require practice. In the course of your research, your dependence on the advice of your supervisor will probably lessen. As writing up proceeds, you can talk on a more equal basis, which makes the relationship stronger again. Sometimes the process of writing up becomes a kind of dialogue between you and your supervisor, with you at each stage achieving a greater refinement of your argument and a more effective presentation of your evidence. You cannot expect to sit down with your data before you and simply rattle off the thesis. It also helps to have more than one sounding board. If you have been allocated a second supervisor, you may be expected to submit your chapters to both. If not, you can still submit those sections to the second supervisor on which she or he is known to have a special interest. If you know a fellow student, not necessarily in your own field, willing to exchange chapters with you, that too can help (though time may be a constraint here, too). When you are working in a second language you may find it helpful to consult a native speaker to ensure that your style is appropriate and easy to follow. All of this takes time, but it is time very well spent since it is easy to boil away the sense in your thesis by expressing yourself poorly.

RESEARCH SCHOOLS

Research students should regard themselves as the backbone of their departments. It is their work after all which looks to the future, providing some of the building blocks from which advances in the discipline will be made. But within an institution research students are usually few in number compared to undergraduates or taught postgraduates and so can feel marginal and overlooked. The development of research schools in UK universities is a move to try to counter this. It ensures there is someone in the governing council of the institution who will speak up for research and who will call for more resources to be devoted to it. Research schools bring together scholars working in cognate fields who may teach within different subject areas or academic divisions within the institution but who share research interests. They and their students become members of the school. This ensures that a sufficient mass forms to make group activities viable and to enable research matters of interest to everyone in the school – seminars, visiting lectures, the provision of study facilities – to be promoted and enhanced.

ENCOUNTERING BUREAUCRACY

Research students tend to be on a relatively long leash. If your research has ranged widely, you may feel that you know external institutions better than you know your own department. This makes relations with secretaries and administrators in the institution of more importance than for taught course students. You will find it helpful to know how to contact your supervisor quickly, how to get help with the various forms which have to be completed (particularly as submission day arrives) and how to get answers to your various questions and concerns. These are all matters which make it worthwhile getting to know the key agents of help and advice in any department, the secretaries and administrative officers. Unfortunately, postgraduate secretarial and administrative staff tend to be amongst the most stretched personnel in the institution. Those dealing with scholarships, grants and student reports are particularly hard-pressed. It helps if you remember this. It is important to be friendly and polite with them, your natural self. You can show them some concern by doing your part to ensure that your forms are returned in good time. Hopefully, you can sometimes approach them with a smile. They in their turn will then ensure that you are not overlooked in the pressure of work but are given the priority and attention you deserve.

SOME QUESTIONS

In undertaking research, what are you looking for from your chosen institution? Supposing that you are not allocated your first choice of supervisor or that she or he moves elsewhere during your studies, what would make you feel still confident that the work could be completed successfully? What relevance for you as a research student has the undergraduate practice of making a timetable for 'free time'?

13 GETTING ADVICE AND SUPPORT

BEING INFORMED

As an international student, you have every reason to want to be well informed. What may appear obvious to domestic students (though in fact they, too, often find university life mysterious initially) may not be entirely so to you. A sensible first stage in embarking on your new studies is to seek for as much information as you can to help you complete your work successfully. In every university and college there are key figures who will be able to answer your questions or point you in the right direction. In fact, though this may not be obvious, the entire institution is structured so as to provide a series of safety nets for you. If you know where they are and why they are there, it might ensure that you only deliberately, and not accidentally, drop into one.

THE STAFF

You are likely to be closest to the teaching staff, usually called lecturers. There are also a number of ancillary academic staff, such as demonstrators and assistants, in the front line of support. Like all staff in the institution, they are there to serve you and you should not hesitate to approach them. But you should give some thought to their needs too. The lecturers are required not only to teach but also to undertake administration and conduct research or do consultancy work. Inevitably, they are often busy. They usually hold office hours, times when they know they will be available to see you, and it is best to try and keep to those. Each of them will be assigned to a secretary and she or he will be able to tell you where to find them and often when they are available to see you outside formal office hours. You may, therefore, first have to find the secretary.

Secretaries

Organisationally the institution is usually broken down into smaller units. The terminology for these varies and you may encounter amongst others some or all of these: colleges, **faculties**, schools, divisions and departments. Each unit, however, will have its main office, which is where the secretaries are based. Whatever course you are studying, you need as a priority to find the main office of the unit. The secretaries are a very important resource for you, indeed for everybody in the institution (which is perhaps why they often feature in academic novels, usually in the role of someone who punctures academic pomposity). They will know the academic staff well and will be able to tell you where all their rooms are. They will also be able to supply you with copies of all the papers about your course (hand-outs, reading lists, course booklets) should you fail to get them in class. And they will be a fount of information about examination dates, essay deadlines, submission arrangements for dissertations and other kinds of information which at some stage you will need to know.

Secretaries, of course, are also busy. They make use of the noticeboard for your course as a way of providing you with information, which you might otherwise have to approach them to acquire. The noticeboard has also been the subject of literary satires, probably again attesting to the fact that it often has real value. So you also need to find the unit noticeboard (which is likely to be in very close proximity to the secretary's office). Before approaching the secretary, you should check that the information you require is not already posted up for you there. But once more you should not hesitate to approach the secretary if you remain in any doubt. You will probably be told at the first meeting of your class (or with your supervisor) about all the people you can contact to help with your work and the information may appear in your course booklet if there is one. Somehow, though, the secretary's importance is often referred to only casually. Don't let this mislead you!

Professors and executive officers

The academic staff has its own grades and hierarchies, running from lecturers, through senior lecturers and readers up to professors. The **professor** is an especially important figure in the UK. Professors are given oversight of an area of academic work. All the lecturers who teach in this area (and all the students taking courses in this area) will see the professor as one of the key authority figures. Above the professors, the chain of command stretches all the way to the head of the institution usually called the Principal. Often, however, this academic hierarchy is paralleled by a more functional one. Some individuals are selected from amongst the lecturing staff to serve in a variety of different executive positions. For example, there is likely to be a course director and perhaps also a leader of a sub-unit or unit of studies with a title like sectional head or chairperson. These are all resources to which you can turn. The best policy is to start at the lowest level and seek information, advice or assistance there. If the person there cannot deal with your enquiry, you will referred up to a higher level and then, if necessary, to an even higher one.

Welfare and confidential support

It is also likely that you will be assigned to a member of the academic staff who will act as your adviser during your time in the university. The adviser will serve primarily for academic advice (course choices, for example) but will also be in touch with the entire range of welfare services within the institution, including counsellors, disability officers, careers staff, health officers and so on. In other cases, the tutor or supervisor will play something like this same role. You are free to consult amongst the academic staff wherever you feel most confident of a sympathetic response. If, however, you wish to talk over something on a confidential basis, and you prefer that your academic advisers should not be informed of this, then there are also professional confidential counsellors available for you to approach. Counsellors are there to help you with any matter which is affecting your studies – personal relationships or family concerns, concerns about your living or working environment, financial concerns, problems with homesickness, health or cultural sensitivities. There are very strict laws in the UK on confidentiality which these counsellors (and indeed all university personnel) will scrupulously respect. Once you have identified the best source of advice for you (your Students' Association will help and you can approach them yourself), you should feel free to be open and frank. The confidentiality laws will also protect you from any unwelcome interference from outside the institution. Your address, for example, is known to the university but is not disclosed to outsiders. If you are requested to set aside that confidentiality, to take part in some experiment, for example, you should be quite certain before agreeing that in your view those making the request will respect and preserve your privacy. You have a right to refuse. But you can also decide for yourself what limitations on your privacy you are prepared to allow.

CAREERS AND EMPLOYMENT

Many students look to their university degree to improve their employment prospects. But most university careers service officers say that students wait too long before consulting them. It is unwise to approach the careers service only in your last weeks of student life as the challenge of employment suddenly looms before you. Much better to make early contact in order to see what the service offers, to consult its library and learn of its practices. Many careers offices have programmes which teach you the techniques involved in finding a job – like preparing a curriculum vitae, for example. Others will offer you advice on the choice of job which might suit you best. Some have 'milk rounds' when representatives of leading employers hold sessions in your university or city and interview all those interested in their line of work. If you have registered with your careers service for this, you will be invited to attend. A careers service in the UK receives information primarily on British jobs. It will also be in touch with employers in the European Union. Not all of these contacts may be suitable for you if you are intending to return home. But the offices also gather some information on jobs in the wider world and should be able to suggest something for you, too. It makes sense to check it out.

INTERNATIONAL OFFICES

Most universities with a significant number of international students will also boast an international office, though it may not bear that name. Whatever it is called, this office will have some responsibility for looking after you during your time in the UK. Usually, it contains people who are experienced in providing advice on a number of issues of major concern to international students, such as immigration matters (how to get your visa renewed, for example). It will also be able to offer advice should you be faced by a difficult situation in your home country. When a recent financial crisis hit a number of Asian countries, it was this office which provided information and counselling to concerned students. The international office is the division in your institution which is in closest touch with matters in your own country. Often, members of the office will visit your country to participate in educational exhibitions, for example. As a result, they will often be able to find things out for you or to put you in touch with those who can provide answers to your questions. It is usually the international office which deals with study abroad and can give advice about opportunities available. And the same office is often in very close touch with other bodies which have a special interest in international students, such as the accom-

modation services, the welfare offices and international societies and clubs. It can, therefore, be used as a one-stop contact
point for all of these.

Some international offices arrange events for the spouses
and children of international students. Sometimes they can
provide information on things like shopping and leisure facilities. Some hold informal language classes for partners who
would like help with their English. Some arrange coffee
mornings, often with crèche facilities, to allow partners to
meet and socialise. For many partners, this can help break the
isolation of life at home with young children in a new
environment. It can also be the basis of forming lasting
friendships between families. But in order to benefit from this
you have first to inform the office that your partner and your
children are with you, which you should do by calling on the
office and making enquiries. Otherwise you may hear nothing
about this. The institution keeps academic records concerning
its students only; it may not even know that you have a partner
with you unless you are prepared to take the initiative and to
pass on the information.

THE LIBRARY

Apart from key personnel, the resource most used by students,
even today when electronic data is so much in vogue, is the
printed word. One of the principal resources is the library – or
learning centres, as they are becoming known in the age of the
computer. The ones in your institution are likely to be far
bigger and far more complex than any you have ever encountered before. You must spend some time in your early weeks
finding out how the library works, how the books are classified, where to find what you are interested in and under what
conditions books or journals can be consulted and borrowed.
If the work you are looking for is not available immediately,
you need to be able to find others closely related to it which
are. The library is also likely to contain reference books, on
study skills for example, which the staff will be able to point

out to you. It is probably enough to be aware of these initially. Then, if the occasion arises, you will remember where to find them.

Libraries, with their enforced silence and serried ranks of serious-looking readers, can be off-putting places. Learning to prize them and to feel comfortable in them must be an early goal. You can walk round the open stacks, get to know what is in the closed ones, practise using the catalogues (particularly any on-line ones), search out a few journals, become familiar with borrowing practices and start borrowing books.

COURSE BOOKLETS

Most courses, both undergraduate and taught postgraduate, have course booklets. These can be particularly illuminating and should be read with care and kept for reference as the course proceeds. Details about the course are often provided (lecture titles, recommended reading lists, a description of how your work is assessed and how it is examined). Many even include guides to study methods (some indication of how essays should be researched and presented, for example). In recent years, under pressure from those investigating university teaching methods, these booklets have often become extremely elaborate. But they are not always as valued by students as they should be. For anyone coming from another country, particularly if you are used to different teaching and study methods, this guide to what to study and how to study should not be ignored.

CODES OF PRACTICE

Another obvious source of assistance which can be helpful to those unfamiliar with UK conventions are the various codes of good practice which universities and colleges now issue. The UK government sees these as the equivalent of service-level agreements. They set out the obligations which the institution accepts towards its staff and students. Postgraduates, for example, are likely to be issued with a published code governing the mutual responsibilities of staff and students in relation to the instruction provided. These codes often specify the assistance available to you. They may detail the procedures which you can invoke if matters go wrong, at examinations, for example. They may outline procedures for how you can make changes if staff–student relationships, particularly between tutor and student, are judged to have broken down. Even if nothing goes wrong and relationships are excellent, the knowledge that the institution has considered these matters and made provision for them can be distinctly reassuring.

COMPUTING SUPPORT

It is essential for every student today to have some understanding of computers and many universities make the acquisition of computing skills one of the transferable skills goals which they set for students. When you first arrive you may well be given an e-mail address and access to the Internet. You will then be expected to consult your e-mail on a regular basis and information of importance about the course or your studies may appear there. In return, it is hoped that you will keep in touch with your tutors, sending a message, for example, when you may have to miss a tutorial. If you can type, you may also be required to prepare your written work (essays and projects) on a word processor. Some institutions enable or encourage international students to form e-mail networks. If adopted by national or international groups, this can create a strongly supportive community for you. A network enables you to keep in touch with others who share a lot of your interests and even to arrange outings on a group basis. It often provides a means by which news and events of particular interest to international students, like local festivals, visiting lectures, sales of books, job interviews and accommodation vacancies, can quickly be publicised.

There are huge advantages to you in becoming computer

literate, if you are not so already. Working on a word processor or computer makes it easy for you to edit and revise your work and will also enable your tutors to offer their comments in a clear and legible form (something not always otherwise to be relied on). It will ensure that your work looks good when submitted, which obviously helps. Computers can check your spelling and grammar, too, which is of great value to those not working in their own first language. Postgraduate students can compose tables and arrange data sets on their word processors or computers and even produce slides and illustrations to support their oral presentations. Computers give you access to the Internet, which is increasingly important for all students, particularly those undertaking research, since a great wealth of research data is now available there. The computer can often also be used to get further information on your studies or access to library catalogues.

Virtually all universities run computer courses for students, usually extending from the elementary to the very advanced. You will probably be offered access to a variety of different computers on campus and the opportunity to learn about different programmes for each of them. This involves an initial investment of time and effort on your part, but it is well worthwhile. Eventually it will save you work and will open up to you means of accessing information and processing your findings which can be extremely valuable in your studies and later on when you get a job. Even a little knowledge can help. If you need technical support, the computing rooms are likely to be provided with expert computer staff to help you with any problem which may arise. It hardly needs saying that they are knowledgeable and that they are aware of the kinds of difficulties which you are likely to face.

ON-COURSE LANGUAGE SUPPORT

Some international students while on their course encounter a problem with language. This is seldom deep-rooted, as institutions have to satisfy themselves that your level of English is acceptable before offering you a place. It is also sometimes confused simply with the difficulty of mastering a greater volume of reading, which all students face. Even so, a few students do find that their level of English understanding makes it difficult for them to follow lectures or to read rapidly enough or to participate easily in tutorials. Most institutions in the UK have a specialist language service which can help. There are also many tape and video programmes available commercially which can be used privately to enable you to enhance your skills. It is also possible to attend an English improvement course outside the university or to get together informally with those who feel they share the problem. Holding a small self-help English discussion group can have social as well as educational benefits. When your institution is aware that you have a problem, it will usually be able to suggest some means of tackling it and will often offer the assistance freely as part of its provision for students. But you may first have to discuss the problem with a tutor or someone else in authority. Most language problems resolve fairly quickly, particularly as you have the stimulus of hearing English spoken all round you all day. But this is not achieved simply by hoping the problem will go away. You have first to take it seriously and get advice.

SPECIAL NEEDS

For students who have or who develop special needs, the key thing is to be aware of the variety of specialist services on offer, from personal counsellors to disability advisers. Institutions are anxious to assist you where they can and often pride themselves on what they achieve. If they have admitted you, they have acknowledged that they will give you every opportunity to succeed. They are also bound by law to make basic provision for students with many different kinds of special need, such as impaired mobility. The Students' Association is usually a source of information about everything which is available and it often provides a guide to services, which can be of great value. It will certainly point you in the right direction. If there is an office with a special responsibility for special needs, it is obviously important for you to register there on arrival (or even before arrival) and then to refer back any problems you encounter routinely. If there is no single office, you are probably best to do this through your academic counsellor. Either way, you will have someone acting on your behalf to ensure that the services you require are in place. Sometimes the facilities will all be in place already. Sometimes you may have to point out what is needed. A regular channel for reporting makes this much easier.

WIDER STUDIES

Many international students want to use their time in the UK to undertake studies outside the classes formally required in order to complete their degree. There are some problems with this when the classes are heavy and demanding, as most university courses are. But the opportunity is certainly there and it can be of huge benefit, as the biographies of international students frequently attest. Most institutions in the UK provide courses for students to gain skills which relate to their main studies. For example, courses on learning a new foreign language or mastering a new computer language will often be available outside the degree structures. In addition, the universities usually offer classes to the public in the form of continuing education or lifelong learning courses which are sometimes open to students, too, on payment of a very small fee. There are also 'community education' classes held on the same basis in local schools and colleges. These quite often offer a huge range of subjects from floral art to finance. They tend also to attract people of different ages and backgrounds, which can add to your contacts locally and your knowledge of UK society. If you would like to and have the time to undertake them, these courses provide an excellent opportunity for you to broaden the base of your knowledge and skills. Some students, for example, find they can pick up things in this way which not only deepen their understanding of their principal studies but open up new avenues of interest or research. Such a programme on top of a full course load can, however, be impossibly demanding and priority has to be given to the degree studies. There is a good deal of evidence that those who do take on too much endanger their progress in everything rather than just in the extra studies they have undertaken. You have to be willing to try things out and to give them up if they prove burdensome.

DISCRIMINATION

Sadly, globalisation, which has fostered developments like the growth in international education, has not been accompanied by the elimination of discrimination. Prejudice by one community against another, one gender against another, one set of beliefs against another is still found in most countries in the world. Most people would argue that, in the UK at least, there have been marked changes within the last generation and a growth in understanding and tolerance generally. The law is now firmly on the side of those who oppose discrimination and those who experience discrimination are much more willing to take action to oppose it. None the less, racism and sexism are still found. If you experience anything attributable to discrimination within or outside your institution, you should report it and get advice from your counsellors on what to do about it. If you intend to seek legal redress, it is likely that there will be constraints (proof in such matters may require witnesses) and you may need to be advised on how to use the law. But a great deal can be achieved even without bringing the law into it. What is important is that you should make the matter known and allow it to be investigated.

Certainly every educational institution in the UK deplores discrimination and tries to ensure that it has policies in place to prevent it. Codes of practice for students and staff will include this. Strong rules now operate, in connection with examinations, for example, which seek to make discrimination difficult if not impossible. If within your institution you experience discrimination in any form or if you feel you are a victim of sexism or racism, you should report the matter at once to someone in authority. They are obliged to record it, have it investigated and to take action to resolve it. You can also take the matter to your Students' Association. You should expect your report to be treated extremely seriously and dealt with sensitively, scrupulously and fairly. If you feel it is not, you can take the matter up the chain of command as far as the principal or **vice-chancellor,** if necessary. Some institutions have appointed an ombudsman (an independent arbitrator whose role is to settle grievances raised by individuals against their institution) for this kind of problem. The Students' Association will be able to advise on the best route for you to take.

SOCIAL INTEGRATION

Many international students will want to get to know something of the people in the country in which they have come to live, not just its students and academics but those in the wider society. This can happen, of course, by attending local societies or classes or joining in local events. But your university may also have programmes in place designed to allow you to get to know local people. Some arrange hospitality programmes, for example, under which people from the local town or city will volunteer to invite a few students home for a meal or a cup of tea or for some other social occasion. These invitations are particularly popular around Christmas or New Year, which is the main season in the UK for families and their guests to get together. There is even a national group which will arrange vacation home-stays for you with UK families in various parts of the country (www.hostuk.org). These opportunities to interact with locals are a good way of meeting a more general cross-section of UK society. They also enable locals to get to know you and the country from which you have come. Sometimes friendships are formed which last long after your study years are over. If these opportunities are available at your institution, the international office (or its equivalent) will be likely to know.

SOME QUESTIONS

Academics often talk of their 'pastoral role'. How could that benefit you? Non-academic staff refer to their 'support role'. What support would you most value?

14 INTERNATIONAL STUDY AND THE INTERNET

All who work in international education are aware of the importance of the Internet. If you surf the net, you can find high quality (and, just as easily, low quality) information at your fingertips. You can use the Internet to survey the entire field of UK **tertiary education**. You can use it to arrange flights and fix up accommodation. You can use it to find out about countries, communities, institutions. The amount of information on the World Wide Web is now almost overwhelming. It is so large, in fact, that students often complain about the time it takes to access a web-site or to download information. In the UK practically all institutions and organisations have their own web-site. Certainly all academic ones will do so. Even many individuals have a site which they use to provide information on their own particular interests or to express their own particular views. Finding your way through this labyrinth is not easy but a few signposts may be of some help.

UK institutions

If you are using the Internet to undertake searches on UK post-school education, where do you begin? The main site for all UK institutions is the British Council one, which can be found at: **www.educationuk.org**.

Education UK is the educational marketing arm of the British Council. As an organisation with close links to the government, the Council often speaks on behalf of the UK as a whole. Its web-site is therefore extraordinarily useful in providing a basic introduction to all aspects of study in the UK. It is also relatively easy to use. You can also use it to find out about such matters as entry clearance, scholarships and pre-course studies. This central service is complemented by web-sites in individual countries where Education UK offices are based. These sites are often in the local language and address the particular needs of local enquirers. Even British Council offices which do not have an Education UK unit may be able to provide information about UK education. The Council operates in 109 countries worldwide and you will find a list of their offices at: **www.britishcouncil.org/where/index.htm**.

There is also a subscription service for institutions. Not all institutions do subscribe, but the web-site is able to include the entire UK educational sector, rather than just individual institutions. This can be found at: **www.hotcourses.com**. There are direct links from the site to every one of the universities and colleges in the UK. As such, it has real value. A few of the sites even provide an online application service. Amongst other features the Hotcourses site offers a search facility, allowing you to look for particular subjects, courses and locations.

If all you need is a list of UK institutions, this can be obtained at: **www.britishcouncil.org/eis/profiles** and for Scotland at: **www.educationukscotland.org**. The latter web-site has the extra value of dealing with Scottish institutions as a whole. These again allow access to the individual web-sites of the institutions, which is helpful once you know where you want to go.

Search engines

If you would like to mount your own enquiries and to make your own approaches, there are a number of search engines which you can use. Perhaps the best known of these are: **www.google.com**; **www.msn.com**; and **www.yahoo.com**. These enable you to find information simply by typing in the name of the subject of interest to you. Inevitably, you may have to put your enquiry in several different forms in order to find what you are looking for: UK education; UK universities; UK colleges; International study; UK study abroad; UK student exchanges – all sorts of headings may be relevant. But this at least opens up an enormous range of information for you and may take you in different directions from those in the official sites.

UKCOSA

Another very valuable web-site is that of the United Kingdom Council for Overseas Student Affairs which can be found at: **www.ukcosa.org.uk**. UKCOSA looks after the welfare needs of international students in the UK. It publishes a large number of pamphlets about such matters of importance for international students as how to find funding, housing, part-time work and so on. These pamphlets are all available at the web-site and can be downloaded from there. The site also gives advice on entry clearance, banking and employment regulations.

UK bodies

The universities and colleges in the UK are organised into national and regional bodies and these also have their own web-sites. The main function of these bodies, however, is to exercise some oversight of all matters academic within their sphere. They are the mouthpieces of executive committees representing the principals. Their web-sites, therefore, offer comments on all major educational issues of the day, particularly those of concern to government and the press. But you can also use them to provide links to the universities and colleges and to other educational bodies.

Universities UK: **www.universitiesuk.ac.uk**
Universities Scotland: **www.universities-scotland.ac.uk**
Association of Colleges: **www.aoc.co.uk**

Quality assurance

Those who want to know about the Teaching Quality Assessments and the Research Assessment Exercise reports in the UK have to look at a number of different sites. For the Quality Assurance Agency for Higher Education: **www.qaa.ac.uk**. This provides the report from the Quality Audits on individual institutions. For Further Education, information can be found at: **www.britcoun.org/education/system/fe/fequality.htm**. For Wales, there is: **www.wfc.ac.uk/fefcw/feqa/index.html**. For Scotland, try: **www.scotland.gov.uk/hmis/fereports.asp**. For the Research Assessment Exercise reports: **www.hero.ac.uk/rae**. This includes the rules and regulations behind the exercise and often the very detailed reports as well as the summaries and assessment methods employed.

UCAS

Applications for undergraduate places go through UCAS (Universities and Colleges Admissions Service). There is both an electronic and paper application process. The web-site is: **www.ucas.co.uk**. The e-mail address for enquiries is as follows: **app.req@ucas.ac.uk**. The UCAS Directory can be found at: **www.swotbooks.com/ucasbooks**. For help on how to complete your UCAS form: **www.careers-portal.co.uk/bookshop**.

Research

For research opportunities and general HE information, see: **www.hero.ac.uk/**. This also has a valuable search facility.

Study abroad

For study abroad, the main European programme can be found at: **http://europa.eu.int/comm/education/erasmus.html**. The

British contact point is: **www.ukc.ac.uk/ERASMUS/**. The best site for programmes for North Americans is to be found at: **www.britishcouncil-usa.org/learning/students/studyabroad/**.

EFL

If you would like to learn about studying English as a foreign language in the UK, there are again a number of sites which might be of help. The following are a selection:
www.learnenglish.org.uk
www.englishinbritain.org.uk
www.bbc.co.uk/worldservice/learningenglish

Qualifications

If you are in search of a guide to British qualifications and how these compare with other qualification systems in the rest of the world, the most used source is NARIC. The NARIC web-site is: **www.naric.org.uk**. E-mails: **naric@ecctis.co.uk**. For Scottish qualifications **www.sqa.org.uk** is useful. E-mail address: **helpdesk@sqa.org.uk**.

Funding

Funding is a major concern for students and here you may have to range very widely. For grants, scholarships and funds, the web-sites for the British Council and for UKCOSA given above offer helpful advice. For British Council awards: **www.britishcouncil.org/education/qdu**.

Employment

For employment issues access the following web-site: **www.dfes.gov.uk/international-students/wituk.shtml**. Information on work permits for those who require them may be found at: **www.workpermits.gov.uk**. For postgraduate studies and careers, see: **www.prospects.ac.uk**; for graduate jobs, see: **www.jobs.ac.uk**.

Visas and immigration

For help with visas, the main site is: **www.ukvisas.gov.uk**. If you need help with immigration and nationality issues, try: **www.ind.homeoffice.gov.uk**, or look up the advice from the Foreign and Commonwealth Office: **www.fco.gov.uk**.

Medicine and dentistry

Medical training and dental training is best approached through: **www.doh.gov.uk/medicaltrainingintheuk** and through: **www.gmc-uk.org** (for doctors) and **www.gdc-uk.org** (for dentists).

Travel and health

Advice for students about travel, getting a driver's licence or going by rail or bus also involves several different sites:
Driver and Vehicle Licensing Agency: **www.dvla.gov.uk**
Train bookings: **www.thetrainline.com**; **www.scotrail.co.uk**
Inter-Rail: **www.inter-rail.co.uk**
National Express (bus): **www.gobycoach.com**
and information about where to go within Britain may be found at: **www.visitbritain.com**.

Finally, if you want more information about the UK weather, try looking up: **www.weather.co.uk**; for information on health matters, look up: **www.nhsdirect.nhs.uk**.

GLOSSARY OF UK ACADEMIC TERMS

Oscar Wilde thought that Britain and the USA had everything in common except language. The varieties of English use in the rest of the world and the fact that American usage is often heard have suggested the need for a brief glossary of terms employed in the UK academic world.

Academia The academic world, usually applied to the universities and colleges as a whole.

Academic As a noun, it means a university or college teacher or lecturer (American 'professor').

Academic year The period from when classes start until the end of the session. Until lately, the UK academic year began in October and was divided into three terms, from October to December, from January to March, and from April to June. In more recent times, a two-semester year has been introduced in some institutions, sometimes following the old term structure but dividing in late January, sometimes based on two new terms, generally running (often with breaks) from August or September to December and from January to May or June.

Assessment The marks or grades assigned for student performance in examinations, essays, projects and other work. Different scales are used in UK colleges and universities, though most relate to honours classifications. There are also standardised scales for the purpose of allowing credit to be transferred internationally. The GPA (Grade Point Average) system is little used in the UK.

Class A single unit and component part of a degree programme or the students who attend it ('a physics class'). When applied to teaching, it is often a synonym for course. When applied to honours degree results, it means one of the three standard grades (first, second, third).

Class examination Part of the overall course assessment. Generally taken at some intermediate point in the period of study. Used in contrast to 'degree examination'.

College An academic institution, usually one with too few students to be regarded as a university or one which concentrates on non-degree courses. The term is also used for some schools and sometimes for divisions of a university.

Course Used mainly for a single unit within a degree programme ('a chemistry course'), usually one lasting a semester or year, but also for the entire programme ('a degree course in chemistry'). Undergraduates generally take several courses a year but in doing so they may be following a single course of studies.

Degree An academic award conferred on students in universities and some colleges. The principal UK degrees, which are generally sequential, are designated bachelor, master's and doctorate. A bachelor degree is sometimes called a 'first' degree.

Degree examination End-of-course test. Degree examinations taken at the end of the entire programme of undergraduate study (after three or four years typically) are sometimes called 'finals'.

Diploma An academic award, usually higher than a bachelor degree but lower than a master's degree and sometimes forming an element of the latter programme. The term is used more generally to refer to any kind of academic award.

Externals Examiners appointed by one university from another to advise on the awards of degrees and on assessment and the maintenance of academic standards.

Faculty A group of cognate departments or allied university teaching units ('the Social Sciences faculty'). The term is never used in the UK in its American sense of administrative and academic staff.

Further education Instruction provided in colleges which offer principally vocational and training courses to students who have completed their compulsory school education (usually from age 16). It is often abbreviated to FE. Some of these colleges also now offer degree courses and the differences between further and higher education are held to be diminishing.

Higher education Instruction provided in universities and colleges which offer principally degree courses to students who have completed their secondary school education (usually from age 18). It is often abbreviated to HE.

Honours	A form of ranked assessment used in some undergraduate degrees. Generally there are three classes, first, second and third, with the second sometimes divided into upper and lower. The system is currently controversial, some authorities arguing that such distinctions have ceased to be relevant in a more egalitarian world, others that they are not discriminating enough to be useful in a less egalitarian world.
Joint degree	An undergraduate programme involving specialisation in more than one subject. Generally, undergraduate students study either for a pass degree (several other terms are used for this) or an honours degree. In the latter case, students generally specialise in either one subject ('single honours') or two or more ('joint or combined honours').
Lecturer	An academic teacher. The same word is also used for the lowest of the grades amongst university teaching staff, the others being senior lecturer, reader and professor. Lecturer, rather than professor, is the term customarily used to refer to academic staff in the UK.
Postgraduate	A student who usually already holds a bachelor degree and who has embarked on a higher level of studies (normally master's or doctoral study). The US term is graduate.
Professor	The highest grade of university lecturer, usually restricted in the UK to a small percentage of the total academic staff. Professors generally have an identified area of particular expertise within their discipline. In a department, they will exercise academic authority over other members of staff and students within this area. But academic authority and executive authority for the running of the department may be separated, so that posts such as course director or head of department may be held by academic staff who do not have the title professor.
Seminar	A discussion group of students and academics. A seminar can resemble a tutorial but is normally larger. It is also more commonly employed in advanced courses. In a tutorial, the tutor may expect to exercise a more directive or controlling role.
Split degrees	A modified form of joint award. Some universities, though not involved with the teaching, will 'recognise' studies taken at other universities (usually overseas) as equivalent to part of their own academic programme. This enables students who have been successful in the overseas institution to transfer directly into the UK one. In fact, most UK institutions do

recognise studies taken at other reputable institutions and some 'recognition' or 'credit' for these studies is often allowed to students who are permitted to transfer. With split degrees, however, 'full credit' is normally conferred.

Tertiary education   A term covering both HE and FE. Strangely enough, it is never abbreviated to TE.

Vice-chancellor   A title often held by the principal or head of a university. Generally, in the UK every university has a titular head who is called the Chancellor, a position often held by members of the royal family or of the House of Lords. The actual executive head theoretically stands in for this titular head on most ceremonial occasions and therefore bears the title Vice-Chancellor. But almost all vice-chancellors (or VCs) also have their own title of Principal, which is regarded as the equivalent of College President in the USA.

ACKNOWLEDGEMENTS

This book is based largely on the day-to-day experience of working with international students as a lecturer and as an international officer. Given the disparate sources which this involves, it does not seem appropriate to include a bibliography, as the other books in this series have done. I would like, however, to acknowledge my debt to a volume in this series, Christine Robinson's *Get Set for English Language*, which formed one starting point. On study skills, I have found the Open University volumes of real value, especially Andrew Northedge's *The Good Study Guide* (Milton Keynes: Open University Press, 1990), and I have long made use of Estelle M. Phillips and D. S. Pugh's *How to Get a PhD*, third edition (Buckingham: Open University Press, 2000). Like everyone working with international students, I also value Christine Humfrey's *Managing International Students: Recruitment to Graduation* (Buckingham: Open University Press, 1999). All are acknowledged as sources here.

I have also to thank a number of people who have assisted me in my work. Amongst many colleagues at the University of Edinburgh, Sandra Morris, Alan Barnard, Kirsty Gillies, Jane Causer, Jim Thompson and Ian Wotherspoon deserve special mention for their help and advice. Nicola Carr, the Commissioning Editor, made it all happen. Rhoda Borcherding of Pomona College in California, Jacqui Allan of the British Council in New Delhi and the anonymous readers who gave a press opinion on my proposal helped me to see the way forward. Jim Strachan provided unfailing support. I would also like to thank the students on the Pomona Programme in Edinburgh, who put up with my questions. All of them and all the international students I've talked to over the years have contributed more than they knew. The views expressed in the book, however, are my own.

INDEX